A Field Guide
for
Incoming Spirits

Conversations About Being Human

I0104479

A Field Guide
for
Incoming Spirits

Conversations About Being Human

Ardeth De Vries

A Field Guide for Incoming Spirits

Copyright 2025 Ardeth De Vries

All rights reserved. No part of this book may be reproduced in any form or by any electronic or mechanical means including information storage and retrieval systems, without permission in writing from the author.

Book design by River Sanctuary Graphic Arts

ISBN 978-1-952194-46-7
Printed in the United States of America

Additional copies available from:
riversanctuarypublishing.com
amazon.com

River Sanctuary Publishing
P.O. Box 1561
Felton, California 95018

www.riversanctuarypublishing.com

Dedicated to the awakening of the New Earth

*This book is dedicated to
all of the people and animals
who have offered many lessons for me
to learn about being human.
I'm a work in progress, still
learning how to walk my talk.*

ACKNOWLEDGMENTS

*T*his book wasn't written in a vacuum. Not even close. Thank you to the following for their help in making *A Field Guide for Incoming Spirits: Conversations About Being Human* a book rather than just an idea in my head:

Annie Elizabeth Porter (co-founder of River Sanctuary Publishing), thank you for your hard work, insights, suggestions, support, and belief in this book. Annie, you're a very classy human being and I value and respect you.

David DiPietro Weiss, also co-founder of River Sanctuary Publishing, thank you for many years of teaching, playing and learning together on this visit. David, you always believed in this book too and even though you aren't physically here any longer, I hope you're smiling about seeing the book in print.

Thank you to Melanie Gendron for creating the beautiful cover for this book. Your spirit shines through your talent.

Celeste Bennett, Marcia Bahr and Bruce Kint, thank you for your editing, suggestions and support.

A BIG thank you to all of the people and animals who have taught me so much about being human.

Contents

Author's Note

My belief system provides the underlying premise of this book so it's important that you know where I'm coming from before you continue, because if you don't understand my bottom line you'll be saying "Huh?" quite often as you read the book.

I believe that this life on Earth isn't my first rodeo. I chose to leave the place I call HOME to avail myself of the opportunities that might exist here which would allow me to learn the lessons I assigned myself when I was HOME. HOME is where I came from and HOME is where I'll go when I've left this body.

Is that too woo woo for you? Hopefully not because this book isn't really woo woo at all. I see this book as being very practical.

This isn't a scholarly work with an extensive bibliography at the end, so if you're looking for something academic this book isn't for you. Even though I'm fairly well educated and reasonably well read in an eclectic sort of way, what I've learned about being human hasn't come from schools or books. I'm not saying that education and reading haven't been valuable, but experience is also a great teacher.

I see this book as a series of conversations between you and me. As I write I imagine that I'm talking with you; maybe we're sitting down and visiting over a cup of coffee or tea. Because we're having a conversation, I'll also be taking liberties with language and grammar to accommodate the casual aspect of me talking with you. I admit that the English teacher in me is having a hard time not editing as if this were a formal approach, but she'll just have to get over herself and lighten up a bit.

This book is also a kind of "hit and run" approach to the topic of being human. Each chapter could be an entire book in itself—and in some cases already is, written by another author with a different approach—but my intent here is to simply stimulate your interest and present a variety of topics for your consideration. I'd like you to think about the ideas I'll present to you and then form your own opinion as to their validity for you. Imagine that you're in line at a buffet, and each chapter is presented as a food you can sample. I hope you've had enough to eat by the time you finish reading. If you find yourself wanting to revisit the buffet to have more of a particular dish, then I'll feel as though I've really given you food for thought. (Forgive the cliché metaphor. I must be hungry as I'm writing this.)

You might wish that you'd been given this field guide when you first arrived, but part of being human involves dealing with limitations, and since most babies don't read there's a time lag to consider. Not to worry; readiness is everything. As a baby you probably didn't need a field guide yet because the spirit in you was running the show, but by now you've probably forgotten why you're here and how to successfully experience being human. This book might come in handy as a way to jog your memory a bit about why you're here, and my words might even help you become a more successful human being.

Here I Am

What's so hard about being a human being?

I've been a human being for 85 years . . . on this visit. My research for this book has taken place every day I've lived on this planet and during every un-moment I've spent in that space between lives, and I'm not finished yet. Being a human being is a work in progress, but I've decided that since the body only lives so long it's time to write down some of the lessons I've learned about being human. Whether or not these lessons will be of value to you is something you'll have to decide for yourself. I can only tell you what's true for me. I'll be delighted if the thoughts presented here resonate with you in any way, but if they don't I'm okay with that too. Just don't stop reading until you get to the end of the book. Who knows what little kernel of insight you may find toward the end that might sound right to you. I'd hate for you to miss a thought that fits for you by closing the book too soon.

One way to think about this book is to imagine that I'm asking you to put together a puzzle. The only difference between the puzzle I'm asking you to arrange and puzzles that you've worked on before is that, in this case, you don't know whether all of the pieces in the box fit together to produce the picture on the front of the box. What's the picture? The picture on the front of the box is an image of you. Pretend that I'm telling you that there are pieces from many different puzzles in the box. You may conclude some pieces don't belong to the puzzle that represents you, but all of the pieces in the box belong together in a montage. What image they produce depends on which pieces fit together. You may discover during this process that you find a piece you really want to use, but you just can't make it fit where you want to place it. You might put this piece aside, thinking that it belongs to a different puzzle, only to come back later on and find that it really does fit. But not where you thought it belonged in the puzzle. There's something to be said about flexibility and thinking outside the box.

Here we are, human beings on planet Earth, struggling to find out who we are, why we're here, and most importantly for many people, trying to get in touch with the spirit in us. We look to religion, philosophy, and whatever else we can find for answers about our spirituality, but we haven't the foggiest idea which questions to ask, and we've convinced ourselves that if we could only be more "spiritual" we'd be fine.

We've missed the point. We *are* fine. The spirit in us is alive and well. It's the human part of us that's incomplete when we arrive on planet Earth. We aren't born with the conscious knowledge of how to be human. As humans we really do struggle. We kill each other. We destroy our planet. In desperation we run off to outer space hoping the answers are out there somewhere. As spirit we do very well, and in fact know exactly what we're doing and why we're here. We know, as spirit, that we're here to experience humanity and to learn what that's all about. We need to trust the spirit in us to lead us in a positive direction. We need to learn how to be human beings and to understand that WE'RE ALL ONE.

You've probably already found that there are many paradoxes to be experienced here on Earth. For instance, you arrived knowing that you're part of a "whole" only to discover that in solid form you believe you're separate and apart from other humans and life forms. You've been told that being an "individual" is important, and somehow you've interpreted that statement to mean that you must consider yourself as being different than other people; yet a part of you needs to feel connected to other people. Confusing at best, isn't it?

Also, as a human you've felt that the life force which came from the very matrix and essence of spirit is here viewed as a limited existence. The human part of us senses that we're part of something larger, but we experience ourselves as limited. Because of this bizarre notion, humans spend an extraordinary amount of time thinking about death rather than experiencing the joy of life within form. What's even more ironic is that in spite of the amount of time humans think about death and dying, we don't know how to do it very well. We need schools for dying and education in the life aspects of death.

Oh, yes . . . time is also within that paradox. Because Earth rotates on its axis and that rotation is observable, humans keep track of this rotation. Once around is called a day, but that concept becomes convoluted because there are different kinds of days: sidereal or star day, solar or moon day, and so it goes. Before taking on solid form you know that there isn't any time. You know that you're participating in the eternal "NOW," but once you become human, you find yourself dominated by the very clocks and calendars humans have created.

Then, there's the paradox of cause and effect versus free will and choice. Because humans are one of the species on earth to have self-consciousness, we like to put concepts into understandable packages for intellectual digest. Some believe that the universe is based on cause and effect; it operates like a large machine with any one effect traceable to its cause, or as some religions would have it, predestination. Everything is orderly. However, along with this view, humans also embrace free will and choice. How to resolve this dualistic set of philosophies is a discussion that has been going on with humans for centuries.

And there's more. These and other paradoxes are what I'll talk about in the following chapters. There's really quite a bit to digest. For instance, did you know that after having made the decision to be in solid form, it's also very important to know what color you wish to be, or which sex? On the holistic level, these kinds of choices don't matter at all, but they certainly set boundaries in the solid world and often become part of the lessons we've come here to learn.

As spirit we really are fine. We know what we're all about, and we're anxious to get on with our experiences. However, once we're born into the "real" world, the paradoxes I've mentioned begin to pile up and we lose sight of who and what we are and end up getting things backwards. It's our humanity that we've come to experience and work through, not our constant grappling and grasping with spirituality that we either think we've lost, or like children in the game of hide and seek, we think we need to find. We can't lose the essence of what we are, and we certainly don't have to hunt for ourselves as if we're lost. We're not going to get demerits if we give our full attention to this world that we've come to experience. In fact, the whole experience might be much more fun if we could relax and enjoy the lessons we've assigned ourselves.

Humanity begs so many questions. In a rich earth world, why are people hungry? Why do we isolate all old people in the same kinds of homogenized environments? Why are all sick people put in the same kinds of places? Why are we violent toward one another? Why? All of these questions and more continually surface as we live our lives. We're supposed to be in a new age, whatever that means. How can we have a new age without a paradigm shift?

The best we can do as humans is to investigate these questions and answer them if we can. After answers come actions. Perhaps our human experience here on beautiful Earth can contribute to the health and well-being of the whole planet. Now, there's a thought. As spirits we already know that whatever we do matters to the "whole." We're not observers out on a pleasure cruise watching humanity. We <u>are</u> humanity, participating in the eternal NOW. Maybe we ought to give our full attention to being human and be comfortable in knowing and accepting our spirituality as the constant in life.

Together we'll take a look at what's so hard about being a human being. When I asked people—many of them over the years—what they thought was so difficult about being human, the answers ranged from "keeping a straight face during sex" to "dealing with other humans." Everyone agreed on certain basic difficulties that will be explored in the following pages. If I've missed something, perhaps it'll come up before I'm finished writing the book. Or, you can write to me and let me know that the field guide is incomplete, and there's more that needs to be added in a revised version. Who knows? This book could go on for a very long time.

But now, get yourself another cup of coffee or tea and let's begin with where we are.

Chapter 1

THE LIVING FIELD

Why not make your experience a complete one
by connecting with the planet?

Now that we're here, perhaps we should first take a look at the place itself and what it is that's so hard about living on this planet. Considering the fact that we have all kinds of choices available in terms of location, having chosen planet Earth is a trip in itself (pun intended) because this isn't an easy planet to deal with in terms of gravity and atmosphere. When you think about it, just walking around is difficult, and some days it's harder than others, as you well know.

Before we go on about Mother Earth, perhaps a note of clarification is in order about the choice idea. When you just read the previous paragraph about having all kinds of choices about location, did you buy that concept? If not, then probably the rest of this book will challenge your thinking a bit because the whole premise is based on the idea that everything is a choice. Everything. We get to choose who we are, where we'll live our lives, and everything about us. I could go on and on in defense of that concept, but there's plenty of literature on the subject, including a little quantum physics if you need a more scientific approach, so I'll just skip any kind of detailed explanation for now. I'll get into the topic of choice a bit later on in the book. Just humor me by accepting the idea that we all indeed have chosen to be here. Right here. Right now. In this place. On this planet . . . although I hear that Jupiter is lovely this time of year.

Why here? Well, that depends on who you are and what you intend to learn. Our choice of location has a great deal to do with what kinds of opportunities we need to generate for ourselves to accommodate our lessons. No, there's no such thing as predestination or karma; nothing is written in cement. The kind of school you choose to attend depends on what kind of education you think you need. You wouldn't chose a technical school if you wanted to be an actor. Mozart wouldn't have chosen to be a native in a remote African village because that life wouldn't have been conducive to composing the kind of music he wanted to create. For those of us who've chosen this planet, part of what we're all about certainly must have something to do with dealing with limitation—both in terms of Earth's atmosphere and geography—as well as the limitations we impose on ourselves with regard to the bodies we choose. For instance, here we are on a planet that's composed primarily of water and yet most of us live on land. Isn't that interesting?

And then there's the problem of just walking around on this planet. The pressure of the air alone amounts to nearly fifteen pounds on every square inch of our bodies, so a person of average stature is exposed to a total pressure of about fourteen tons. No wonder there are days when just the effort of moving is a bit much. It is true that the air penetrates the porous tissues and cavities of the body, which means that the pressure is exerted equally in all directions, but the pressure still exists even though we're not conscious of it under normal conditions.

We've opted to live on a planet that's rather like a giant gyroscope that tilts and spins on an invisible axis around and around the Sun. One rotation on the axis is considered to be a day, and one revolution counts as a year. Fascinating information, especially since there isn't any time. But that's another chapter.

Another thought about choosing Earth as our living field that's interesting is our relationship (or lack of it) with the planet. I know that we think of relationships as being with other living beings, and I'll talk more about that in another chapter, but have you ever considered your relationship with Earth? Do you even think you have a relationship with this planet? Is it just a place to be? If so, perhaps that's part of the difficulty we often feel about being here. If we don't feel that we have any kind of relationship with the place we call home, our living is compromised by that lack of connection. The earth is alive, after all. There's energy in everything on this planet.

Think about the houses in which you've lived and then expand that thought. Some houses feel like homes, and others simply provide shelter. Do you feel more comfortable in the houses or apartments that you decorate and make your own as compared to those that simply contain furnishings that allow you to sleep, eat, and engage in your life activities?

If you don't establish a connection with your house in some way that place of residence will be simply that and nothing more. People who come into your home should be able to see you in every piece of furniture, wall hanging, and decoration; if they can't make that connection, then you don't live there. Not really. You exist there and the living part has somehow become lost in the shuffle.

As I write this I'm reminded of an apartment I rented after I had just graduated from college. The décor, if one can use such a word to describe a place that was really only one room, was probably a combination of Early Thrift

Shop and Left-Over Attic. There wasn't much to the place. I did, however, feel the need to make the place my own. So, without consulting the landlord, (an oversight that cost me money later on) I proceeded to paint the apartment to get rid of the warm oatmeal color that seemed to permeate everything in the room. One wall became a vivid rainbow of colors; another wall blossomed with many different kinds of flowers; a third wall morphed into a mural depicting the ocean, and the fourth wall grew trees of all shapes and sizes. I'm not an artist, so the visual representation of what I saw in my head was a bit like Salvador Dali meets Picasso without any talent in evidence, but I liked the results. When people came to visit, after a stunned silence, most of them smiled and said that what I'd done with the place was certainly…unique. They were being polite, of course, but no one doubted that I lived there. What my wall paintings meant in terms of being a reflection of who I was became lost in translation, but I'd made my connection with my living space.

Expanding the above thought, the same comment can be made about your relationship with this planet. Earth is a geographical smorgasbord of trees, dirt, rocks and water, but do you feel connected to any of it? I know I must sound like a throwback to the '60's when hugging a tree was the recommended way to connect with nature, which is really not a bad concept, but I'm talking about more than just touching. I'm talking about walking on a beach and feeling one with the sand, rocks, and water. I'm talking about knowing that you're a part of what you're experiencing. It's all about being alive. It's all about knowing that the sand you feel on your feet is a part of you, just as is the water that gets you wet if you walk too close to the shore. Mystical nonsense? No, I think not. There's nothing mystical about being earthy.

Are you familiar with the work of Andy Goldsworthy? If not, there's a DVD you need to watch called "Rivers and Tides." Seeing Goldsworthy work with earth, rocks, and water is an extraordinary experience. This man knows how to connect with the planet, and what he sees and feels will inspire you to open your eyes and senses to Earth in a way that is nourishing and exciting. I promise you that you'll never look at Earth in the same way after you watch this beautifully photographed tribute to the place and the man who shares his creations with the land and water.

Earth is not just a place to be. It's a place to feel and to experience. You chose to be here. You knew, when you were in that space between lives that I call Home, that this planet offered you an opportunity to learn what you wanted to learn. There are lots of other places to be—Earth was not your only choice—but you chose to come here. Why not make the experience a complete one by connecting with the planet?

Are you wondering how to make that connection? Simple, but not easy. Our ability to connect—whether it's with people, animals, or the earth—is often contaminated by what we're thinking. Sometimes we're too busy thinking to just be. Thinking is a vastly overrated activity. Feeling, on the other hand, is another experience entirely. We often talk about losing ourselves in our thoughts, and sometimes we use the expressions, "My mind is wandering," or "I'm losing my mind." It might be better if we let our "mind,"— whatever that is—just wander off sometimes and focus instead on what we're feeling.

Think about the times when you've felt truly connected to something or someone. I'm not talking about the exchange of ideas, which can often be stimulating and you experience a "meeting of the minds" with another person. That's fun, but it's just an intellectual exercise. I'm talking about **feeling** connected. I'm talking about the certainty that comes with feeling you're so close to another living being that you don't feel separate from them. You've experienced this; I know you have. No, I'm not talking about sex. I'm talking about the intimacy that comes with feeling that you're in synch with some other living being. During that moment no words are necessary because you just know that you are one with whatever or whomever you've established that connection.

I share my life with five dogs: Molly, Zuleia, Tamblynn, Inari, and Nyleeria, and we're connected to one another in ways that I can't effectively explain with words. If you've ever loved a dog, cat, horse, or any other animal, you know exactly what I'm talking about don't you? My dogs and I communicate with each other through a kind of intuitive knowing that makes words unnecessary most of the time. They know what I'm thinking and feeling, and I listen to them with the same degree of intensity and comfortableness that I do with humans. Because of our connection with each other, we're extensions of one another. I don't know where they leave off and I begin. I like knowing that we're so connected because that knowledge reinforces what I believe to be important as I live this life. This is what needs to happen in order for us to really be fully present on this planet. We need to feel connected in some way to everything and everyone around us. In order to accomplish this most important task, we need to feel rather than think. Why? Our feelings influence the outcome of the experience.

Many years ago my late partner and I planned to build a new home. In our search for property we found many beautiful places, but none of them felt exactly right until we discovered the piece of ground on which this home now rests. When we came here and connected with the land and the trees that grow like ageless sentinels in this spot we felt that we were home. We didn't know it. We felt it. We opened ourselves to the possibilities that living here would present to us. We chose this place and became a part of what it had to offer us, and what we had to offer it in return.

That's what we need to do with this planet. We need to call it ours and tend this extension of ourselves as we would a child or animal. We need to see ourselves as stewards of the land. If we're willing to be one with the planet on which we've chosen to live, then the outcome of that connection will be that both the planet and we thrive. If, on the other hand, we see ourselves as owners rather than caretakers, then . . . well, you know what happens. You see resistance happening every day. Every time humans try to dominate the earth, the planet shudders and asserts itself in the only ways it knows how. Eventually we'll destroy our living field if we don't listen up and feel the connection we came here to experience.

Chapter 2

THE SUIT OF ARMOR

Being human and living in a body can be
a very satisfying experience.

When we choose to occupy a body we're making a very difficult choice. Stuffing our spirit into an organism that contains 100 trillion cells that move in concert with over 200 bones, complex tissues, assorted organs, and various other systems is a bit like being a one-person orchestra. Imagine billions of microscopic instruments, each with its own sound, playing together in an organized way to produce one piece of music. What's even more amazing is that not only are we the orchestra, we're also the conductor. We decide how the music is to be played.

We're in charge of our bodies—stewards of the armor—just as we're stewards of the planet. No one else is responsible for how we function within our bodies. We're not mindless puppets whose strings are pulled by someone or something else. Our brains contain over ten billion nerve cells that *we* orchestrate. I'd hardly call that being mindless

… although I'm not entirely sure that the mind is really contained in the brain. I think our minds exist inside and outside of ourselves, but that concept is a different book written by someone else.

I know that it's tempting to think that our bodies can be nurtured by outside forces. We look to medicine to fix the broken parts, and we depend on medical people to tell us what's "wrong" with us. Oh, certainly an x-ray can tell a physician that your arm is broken, and that broken arm can be put into a cast to help it heal, but you're in charge of the healing. As much as we like to think otherwise, mind, body, and spirit all function as one unit. It's impossible to separate them. We're in charge of our health and everything else about our bodies.

As babies we learn to live in our bodies and to understand how to use the various parts to our advantage. As we grow older we become more comfortable with the suit of armor we've put on at birth, and as we continue to experience what it's like to be human we also forget where we came from and why we're here. We get distracted. For many people the distractions produce a kind of abdication. Absentee landlords spend most or all of their time away from the buildings they own, and sometimes the premises fall into a state of neglect and disrepair because no one's home to tend the building.

This analogy can be used to describe a condition that I call "being in your body backwards," or not really being in your body at all. This is a very odd kind of circumstance considering the fact that we chose the body we inhabit. We chose our bodies, with all of their genetic qualities and complicated instruments, because these particular bodies are the ones we felt would afford us the best opportunity to learn what we've come here to learn. For reasons that may not be clear to us as humans, we decided that being in a body was important to us. Why then do we neglect the body that we call our own? Are we a bit like the absentee landlord in that by abdicating we hope that someone else will take care of it? Or perhaps we don't care much about our bodies. The physical manifestation of who we are is just a suit of armor after all. Armor rusts, though, if it doesn't get used and maintained. The next time your body feels "creaky" you may want to consider why it might be rusting.

It would have been easy to remain in that space between lives existing as pure energy and total spirit. When we're Home we have no bodies to limit our movements; we can be wherever we wish to be. We have no need for clothes to keep us warm, food to keep us healthy, exercise to keep us fit, or any other kind of human need based on bodily functions. We simply are. Why then would we leave such a seemingly perfect state of being?

Why indeed? Maybe in order to learn what we've assigned ourselves in terms of lessons we need to learn to live with limitations and to rely on a body. Or, what about the idea of just enjoying our bodies? Why can't we do that? Bodies allow us the tactile sensations that aren't possible as spirit. Maybe part of what we're here to learn is to take full advantage of the physical form in all of its splendor. Being human and living in a body can be a very satisfying experience.

How then do we make being human a wonderful experience? How do we celebrate our human-ness? How do we make the suit of armor a part of all that we are?

A famous Star Trek phrase, "Resistance is futile," is applicable to what often goes wrong with the connection we have with our bodies. We do resist sometimes. Often we dislike our earthly forms and try to resist whatever is going on with our bodies. That resistance really is an exercise in futility because we're in charge of everything that goes on with our bodies. Everything.

What would happen if we replaced resistance with acceptance laced with a healthy dose of joy? What would happen if we chose to take full advantage of our bodies and celebrated the many intricacies that allow them to function harmoniously with our spirit conductor?

Before you race off to join an exercise club so you can transform the body you dislike into one that looks like a well-oiled machine, let me say that I'm not talking about creating the "body beautiful" here. At least not in the sense you might think. What I'm talking about is understanding and accepting that you're in charge of your body. You chose to be born into this particular body for a reason. Most bodies aren't "perfect" in any typically observable sense, although I'm not sure I know what being "perfect" really means. Perfection is, after all, a pretty relative term. Imperfections on a physical level often lead to realizations that can be marvelous lessons, either for others or us.

Many years ago I worked with children who spent most of their time living in the oncology ward of a big city hospital. I was supposed to be counseling them and helping them to deal with their imperfect bodies. Actually, they didn't need my help on that level at all. Most of them knew and accepted the fact that they wouldn't survive their illness in this life, but the view they presented of themselves was far from being trapped in imperfect bodies. They wanted to play, laugh, tell stories, and in general, they wanted to be kids.

I remember one little girl in particular who was very sad one day when I came to visit. When I asked her why she was unhappy she said that her parents had just left the hospital and she was sad because they wouldn't play with her. She went on to say that they were so worried about her treatment and frustrated about the inability of the physicians to cure her that she felt they weren't really seeing her. She said she felt very lonely. I asked her what she needed from other people, particularly her parents, and her answer was one I've never forgotten. She said, "I need for people to see me as a whole person, not just as a sick kid."

I don't remember how old this little girl was in earth years, but she was one of the wisest people I've ever met. She knew that her illness was just one manifestation of who she was. She didn't like being ill, but in that wonderful way children have of putting everything in perspective she understood that she needed to play. She knew that she needed to laugh and to enjoy life. So what if she had all kinds of tubes sticking out of her body. So what if she was bald. In a very weird kind of way she was perfectly comfortable in a body we would view as being imperfect and unhealthy. The resiliency of her spirit was inspiring.

I also remember a young boy with whom I spent time on that same ward. One day when I came to visit he deftly maneuvered his wheelchair over to me as I entered the room and asked me if I would do something for him. My answer was, of course, "Sure, Jeremy. What would you like me to do?"

"I want you to buy me a red tee shirt that says, "Bald is Beautiful.""

I laughed and said that I'd get him one that afternoon.

He grinned at me with that kind of wonderful grin you can get from a kid who has a secret and wants you to ask him what it is.

"So, Jeremy, why do you want me to buy you this tee shirt?"

Satisfied that he'd reeled me in, he said, "Because some kids from school came to visit me yesterday and I could tell that they thought I was really ugly because I'm bald, but they didn't say that out loud. I just knew that's what they were thinking. They'll come back, because I asked them to, and when they come again, I want to be wearing that tee shirt."

"What kind of reaction are you looking for?"

"I want them to laugh and maybe even ask me if I feel funny about having a bald head. I want to be able to talk to them about it. I don't want to have to watch them try not to look at me."

"Okay. I get it. Do you really think bald is beautiful, or are you just trying to make a joke so your friends won't feel uncomfortable?"

"Well, yeah, why wouldn't bald be beautiful? What's wrong with being bald? I see lots of adults who are bald

28

and nobody thinks they look weird. I know why I'm bald and I'm okay with it. I've got stuff going on with my body that makes me look different than other people, but I'm the guy living in my body, and no matter what I look like I feel beautiful. I know guys aren't supposed to be beautiful, but you know what I mean. It's just how I feel. Cool, huh?"

Very cool indeed.

Another aspect of living in a body is dealing with the body's need to be fed. This is a pretty basic concept, but we do seem to get in a lather about food sometimes. I've often heard the phrase, "You are what you eat," and I always find myself smiling when I hear those words because my often twisted imagination immediately conjures up images of people who look like French fries, broccoli, or my all-time favorite, Twinkies.

Our twenty-first century culture seems obsessed with food, as witnessed by the fact that there are thousands of books on the market that present a myriad of philosophies about "eating right." Each new book offers a different and often contradictory way of approaching food: all vegetables are good for you; don't eat white vegetables; peanut butter is a good source of protein; peanut butter causes cancer; red wine is good for your heart; alcohol of any kind is bad for you . . . on and on.

Here's an idea: what if we just listened to our bodies and ate according to what our bodies tell us they need? Listen to our bodies? Sure, why not? You listen to your stomach growl and know that you're hungry don't you? Haven't you ever had a craving for a particular kind of food? Where does that so called craving come from? It's a message from our bodies, but sometimes we aren't listening. The absentee landlord example could be used in this context too. Sometimes the pace of our lives is so fast that we just eat and run without paying any attention to the engine that we're fueling. If you're tuned in to your body (remember that you're the conductor too and it's your job to be tuned in to the orchestra) you might find that what you choose to eat to feel healthy takes on a kind of pattern that works very well for you. If you don't eat enough you get a headache. If you eat too much sugar your body has a hard time processing the excess and you feel queasy. If you eat too many fried foods your gall bladder rebels. If fruits and vegetables are words you only use to describe what other people eat, then your ability to fight infection will be compromised. You get the point; I know you do. Just know that you need to pay attention to what you put into your body. Everything that enters your body becomes a part of you, and whether that fuel helps you to function as a healthy person is up to you.

The idea of listening to our bodies can also be applied to various physical symptoms we sometimes experience. I believe, as do many other writers who have devoted whole books to the concept, that there's a direct correlation between what is going on with us physically and what is also going on with us mentally and or emotionally. If you have an earache perhaps there's someone in your life who's trying to tell you something that you don't want to hear, or if your eyes bother you maybe there's something going on in your life that you don't want to see. If your back or legs bother you, are you unwilling to move forward?

Is the congestion in your head being caused by confusion in your mind or heart?

I could go on, but you get the idea. Listen to your body.

Okay. We're here, living in bodies. That makes us human beings living on Earth. What's next? I think it's time to talk about how we function as humans, and that means I'm finally going to address the topic of choice. I've mentioned the word so many times already you've probably become very annoyed with me and wish I'd get on with explaining how the choice concept works. I can't promise you that you'll like the explanation, but then that will be your choice.

Chapter 3

IT'S ALL ABOUT CHOICES

Living your life with an awareness that you're
in charge of you and you're responsible for every choice
you make can be a very liberating experience.

I've already mentioned that before we're born and after our bodies die we exist in that space between lives I call Home. I don't know where that space is; it's probably right here, perhaps in a different dimension. Or not. I don't think it's important to know where Home is, only that it exists. When we're Home we exist as pure energy/spirit. In this space there is no time, and everything about all of our lives is clear to us. It's also a place of reflection and resolution where we think about what we wish to learn and then consider the best possible opportunities to learn the lessons we've chosen for ourselves.

The choices begin when we're Home. Well, "begin" isn't really the right word to use because I believe we live forever, so there really isn't any beginning; however, for purposes of discussion I'll stay with the word I've used.

When we're Home we decide what we wish to learn in our next expression of spirit, and then we choose the best possible time, place, and vehicle for that learning. Sometimes we choose to remain Home as pure spirit; sometimes our choice is to stay Home and function as a guide to someone who has chosen an incarnation elsewhere, and sometimes we choose to be born in a body here on Earth.

As an aside, I should say that even though we make the choice to be born here, we don't separate ourselves from Home. Our spirit, soul, or whatever word works for you, always remains at Home, and regardless of where we are physically we're always connected by a kind of psychic umbilical cord to that part of us that remains Home. That's reassuring isn't it? I like knowing this because I don't feel quite so much like I've set myself adrift here on Earth without being connected to Home.

Let me share one other thought before I go on to talk about the choices we make as humans. I'll use myself as an example: I chose to be born as Ardeth De Vries on June 5, 1940 in Chicago, Illinois. The various paths I've taken as I've experienced this life were not decided by me when I was Home. I only knew that experiencing life as Ardeth De Vries would afford me the opportunities to learn the lessons I chose for myself. The only signposts on the road are those that I've placed there myself. Certainly I'm being

influenced by my spirit self, but the human me is impro-
vising as I go along. Nothing has been predestined. Every
choice I make is one for which I am responsible. I'm not
doing a dance choreographed by someone or something
else; I'm the choreographer of my own dance. Every step
I take is one of my own choosing. Sometimes when I feel
really connected to that part of me that's Home I feel clear
about what I'm doing; on occasion I even understand the
why behind the choice, but the dance is flexible and I can
change steps any time I choose.

Understanding and accepting that everything in life is
a choice also means we're responsible for the choices we
make and the consequences that occur as a result of those
choices. The responsibility factor is a tough one because
even though we often are willing to accept responsibility
for what we might call our "positive" choices, it's not always
easy to accept responsibility for "negative" choices. When
we choose to do something that turns out well, at least
from our perspective, we tend to think that we've made a
"good" choice. Conversely, when we make a choice that has
a "bad" outcome we're not so quick to claim responsibility.
To own choices that result in something not to our liking
somehow makes us sound masochistic, or we come across
as being self-destructive.

Look at choices this way if you will. There are no "good" or "bad" choices. We make decisions based on what we think or feel is the best course of action at the moment. When I was younger I made some choices that I look back on now and wonder what I was thinking. I even make those same kinds of choices now that I'm older because age isn't necessarily a determiner of wisdom. Sometimes the experiences of others can be used as a guide for our own choices, but more often than not we travel our own paths making choices that seem appropriate at the moment. If the outcome isn't what we hoped it would be then perhaps re-visiting the choice and the reasons for the choice might be helpful.

Let's move out of the abstract for a moment and take a look at choices that are more specific. I'm suggesting this approach because I know that on an intellectual level you may find yourself agreeing with some of what I've just said because in theory it's very "adult" to say that you're responsible for your choices, and most of us do aspire to at least sound like adults. Being responsible is a concept we teach our children; we can hardly do less as adults. Let's apply that thought on a more specific level.

What if you're standing on the corner minding your own business and a car hits you? What if you're waiting in line at the bank and you're shot by someone robbing the bank? What if you have a life-threatening illness? Do all of the above questions relate to what we call "accidents" or events beyond our control and therefore become off-limits in a discussion about choices? Why would you choose to get hit by a car? Why would you choose to get shot? Why would you choose to develop a life-threatening illness?

In order to answer the above questions I need to remind you that everything is a choice. Everything. There are no accidents. There are no victims. You chose to stand on that corner. If you hadn't been there the car wouldn't have hit you. You chose to be in line at the bank; if you hadn't been in the bank at the time of the robbery you wouldn't have been shot. You chose your illness because you're in charge of your body.

I know. Now you don't agree with my responsibility premise at all. You're thinking that what seemed reasonable in the abstract isn't reasonable at all in reality. (Whatever that is.) It can't possibly be reasonable to choose to put yourself in harm's way or to choose to be ill, can it?

Perhaps the key to understanding and accepting what I'm saying here is to think about choices in a broader sense and not to attach value judgments to them. Also, it's important to remember that we function most of the time on a conscious level, and yet many of our choices are made from a subconscious perspective. Our subconscious mind—that part of us that we don't understand very well and often don't feel very connected to—is the guiding force behind the choices we make.

What if those choices are a way to learn what we've come here to learn? What if the time spent in the hospital recovering from the injuries you sustained by getting hit by the car or getting shot in the bank offers you time to reflect on what's going on in your life and to re-evaluate your priorities? You've given yourself a "time-out" to look at your life differently. What if, while you're in the hospital, you meet a nurse who later becomes your wife? What if your life-threatening illness is a wake-up call that allows you the opportunity to live your life another way . . . if you choose to do so? What if your illness offers your friends and family an opportunity to re-evaluate their priorities and look at the quality of their lives?

Do you see what I mean by there being a broader context here? Sometimes that broader context only relates to us and how we're living our lives, but often the broader context involves giving other people an opportunity to learn a lesson too. We are, after all, all connected. There are no guarantees that other people will learn from the lessons we offer to them, nor is there any guarantee that you will learn from the lessons you present to yourself, but we do make the choices that set up the opportunity to learn.

There's also what I call the "abdication factor" to consider. Sometimes people are unwilling to make choices because they're afraid that they'll make the "wrong" choice, and so they leave the choice up to someone else. To use a rather mundane and superficial example, you could allow your restaurant companion to order for you because you can't make up your mind what you want to eat, but what if you don't like what your friend has ordered for you? The food placed in front of you is a direct consequence of your "non-choice," and if you don't like the meal that's your problem. As you take the first bite of something that isn't to your liking you might be thinking, "I should have made my own choice." Yep. If you allow other people to make choices for you, then you'd best live with those choices. In the long run it's just less complicated to make your own choices.

Living your life with an awareness that you're in charge of you and that you're responsible for every choice you make can be a very liberating experience. This kind of "I'm in charge of me" mentality allows you to take charge of your life and to be fully present as a competent human being.

But there's more. The effect of believing that you have choices about everything that happens in your life creates a feeling of power within you, and you'll find that your self-esteem increases. Why wouldn't it? People who get this concept have told me that the quality of their lives changed dramatically once they recognized that they were in charge of everything about themselves because they were able to remove the sign pasted to their foreheads that said, "Victim."

Knowing that you're in charge of you also leaves no room for excuses, blaming, or any other kind of "it wasn't my fault" thinking. This realization is also not much fun sometimes because it's often hard to own up to your choices. Playing the victim can be enormously powerful as an attention-getting device, but it's without substance in terms of learning lessons unless your intent when you came here was to experience the emotions associated with being called a victim. There's that too.

Sometimes we choose lessons for ourselves that might be called negative experiences. These so called negative experiences often represent patterns in our lives, which I'll talk about in a later chapter. Patterns are important, but they also can be changed. How many negative experiences do you need to chalk up before you say, "Okay, I get it"? Some people live an entire lifetime here before they're finally ready to release the negative experiences and move on to something more positive, but if what I've just said sounds like it might relate to you, don't feel like you need to continue experiencing life in a negative way if you're ready to make some positive choices. When you're ready to leave the negative and move on to the positive depends on what you've chosen to learn and how much time you feel you need to live the experiences that are a part of the lessons being learned. Your choice.

We are always where we want to be, doing what we want to do, being who we are. If you have a bumper sticker on your vehicle that reads "I'd rather be skiing," then my question to you is simply, "Why aren't you?"

The quality of our lives depends on so many factors: where we live, our parents, friends, wives, husbands, lovers, our jobs, and on and on. We choose all of that too. Sure, we do. Who else does? Who else is responsible for the fact that you have the job you do? Or that you live in Trenton, New Jersey. Many people feel that they have no choice with regard to jobs and many other facets of their lives, but choices always exist. For the man who married young and now has five children, a mortgage and more bills than he can count, life seems without choices. He feels locked in: "If I didn't have a family, I could . . ." "I'd like to change jobs but I need the money." The choices are all there as they always have been, but the consequences and alternatives have become complicated.

We tend to be greedy and impatient. We want every-thing now. To say to the man with five children that he could change jobs if he wanted to would bring forth a volley of "Yes, buts." Sometimes we recognize the choices, but we're not sure that we like the alternatives. I think we know that we can make changes, but it's scary to think about change sometimes because we're afraid that we'll make a mistake, or that people won't like, accept, or understand us. Also, there are many lessons to be learned as we live with the consequences of the choices we've made. In fact, I've come to believe that sometimes we make choices that don't seem appropriate in hindsight because the lesson for us is all about how we deal with the consequences of those choices.

Bottom line? We're responsible for ourselves and our choices. We can change the quality of our lives any time we want to do so. Whether we choose to make changes is often a case of readiness, but sometimes we're unwilling to make changes because the consequences become complicated because other people are involved. Being concerned about other people is admirable, but we aren't responsible for other people, only for ourselves. I'm not saying that we shouldn't take other people into consideration when we make choices, but to use other people and their possible reaction to the choices we make as an excuse is a cop-out. I'm not talking here about the choices we make out of concern for the welfare of others, such as choosing to care for someone who is ill, but rather those choices we make because our major consideration is how others will react to our choices. Big difference. We can't control how other people respond to the choices we make, but we often delude ourselves into thinking that we can as a rationalization for not making a change. Clear communication is the key here when your choices involve other people, and that brings me to the next chapter.

Hopefully you'll choose to continue reading.

Chapter 4

COMMUNICATION

… you really need to think about what you want to accomplish when you communicate with someone.

When we function as human beings most of us don't live in a vacuum. Friends, lovers, spouses, acquaintances, fellow workers, children, animal companions, and various other living beings share our world. We connect with others in many different ways depending on our relationship with them. The common factor involved in all of our associations, whether we're talking about the clerk at Safeway, your spouse, your partner, your children, your friend, or your animal companion, is that we communicate with all of them. Interaction generally involves some form of communication, and this aspect of being human is often very tricky for people. When I talked with people about what's most difficult for them about being human, communication was always at the top of everyone's list. Judging from the number of books on the market that deal with communication, this very human necessity is a problem for many people. Why?

Why is clear and accurate communication such a challenge for many people? Why can't we just say what we mean? Why are we often less than truthful in our communication with others? Why are we able to communicate well with some living beings and not others? What's the big deal?

The big deal, at least from my point of view, involves a consideration of several aspects of being human: often we have hidden agendas; sometimes our ego gets in the way; we want other people to like and accept us so we tailor our communication to accomplish this goal; we aren't sure exactly what thoughts we want to communicate; we just plain aren't interested in communicating; our filter systems cause us to miscommunicate; we aren't listening; or the intensity of our emotions compromises clear communication. Let's take the above considerations and look at what's up with each of them.

Many times when we communicate with people we have a **HIDDEN AGENDA** of our own that influences what we say and how we say it. Because our agenda is hidden, the other person often has no clue what the real message is behind our words. If, for example, you have a decision to make and you ask someone for advice, the other person might not know that you may already have made your decision, and what you really want out of the conversation is for the person to whom you're speaking to agree with what you've already decided. This isn't always true, of course, because sometimes when we ask for advice we really do want to hear what someone else has to say, but in my experience this objective questioning doesn't occur all that often. If you've already made up your mind (even though you may not consciously know that you have) and the person with whom you're communicating doesn't come up with the "right" answer you'll find yourself playing "Yes, but" with them. They won't have a clue why you've responded as you have and the whole conversation will fall apart. If your hidden agenda is that you simply want someone to validate what you're thinking or feeling, then make that clear at the beginning of the conversation so the person to whom you're talking knows what the rules are. Once people know what your expectations are they can decide how to respond. The easiest way to avoid the hidden agenda avalanche of misunderstanding is to be clear in your own mind about what you need from the other person before you even begin conversing. If it's a decision-making kind of conversation, really think about whether in fact you already have made up your mind before you ask for advice. Hidden agendas are trouble no matter how you rationalize them.

EGO is also a biggie for many people. How you feel about yourself makes a huge difference in your communication patterns with other people. If you're really fragile in the ego department, your communication with others will look like a constant search for the holy grail of compliments. If, on the other hand, you're okay with who you are, then whatever someone says in answer to the question or situation you've presented will simply be just another opinion which you can use or discard depending on your needs at the moment.

"PLEASE LIKE ME" is something adults don't generally say to one another. That honest bit of need only works with kids who are generally much more up-front than we are about needing people to like them. Doesn't mean that we don't have those feelings though. A need to be accepted by others is part of being human, and we often spend a great deal of time and energy trying to make other people like us by agreeing with what they say by "brown-nosing," or just plain groveling. You might want to look at how you feel after you've had one of these "Please like me" conversations. You know the answer; I know you do.

Then there's the **CLUELESS COMMUNICATION** that occurs when you're not really sure what you want to accomplish and that uncertainty causes you to ramble and be unclear in what you're saying. Sometimes we just like to hear the sounds of our own voices, and if you ramble on with someone who needs a more succinct kind of verbal exchange you'll find that the end result isn't fun for either of you. You'll feel that the person to whom you're speaking doesn't get what you're saying, and the other person will wish that you'd just stop talking and move on.

SOMETIMES WE'RE JUST NOT INTERESTED IN COMMUNICATING. It's not that you don't like the person talking to you, but at that moment you may not want to talk. For whatever reason. Could be a serious case of avoidance if the subject matter is a difficult one for you, or you may just need to be alone with your thoughts because you're not ready to verbalize them. In any case, if you're having a "I don't want to talk about it" moment, best you avoid situations in which you're likely to be asked an opinion or to offer your thoughts.

We each have what I call our own **FILTER SYSTEM** when we're listening and talking. What we hear and how we respond to what is said to us depends on what's up with us. If, for example, you've just experienced a serious snafu in your relationship with someone, listening to someone else talk about their relationship with their significant other could be compromised by your own experience. What is said and what you hear are often two different things. Everything that comes to us is filtered through our own experiences, judgments, and feelings. For example, I have very strong emotional responses to people who chain their dogs up in the backyard, and so I know that if someone tells me that they chain their animal I'm not going to be in the least bit objective about what their reasons are for indulging in this irresponsible behavior. See, I can't even describe the behavior to you without using a negative adjective. Our filter systems are a part of being human, but they often get in the way of clear communication, especially when strong feelings are involved in the communication process.

Another obvious but sometimes overlooked factor involved in the communication dance has to do with **LISTENING.** How would you assess your listening skills? How carefully do you really listen to what someone else is telling you? If you're going to have a successful dialogue with someone, both of you need to listen to each other. Sometimes we think we're listening, but we really aren't paying attention at all. Why not? Lots of reasons: perhaps you're thinking about something else; or maybe a comment made by the person to whom you're talking triggered a landslide of memories and before you know it, you're wandering down memory lane instead of listening; or, you could be so busy thinking about what you're going to say when the other person stops talking that you don't listen to what they're saying; or ... you can supply any number of reasons here that might be true for you. If you want to communicate successfully, you do need to listen.

One of my favorite annoyances has to do with doctors that don't listen to their patients. Sometimes they're too busy reading charts or thinking that they know what the problem is to really hear what the patient is saying to them. Have you had this experience? If you have, you know exactly what I'm talking about here. The next time you see a doctor, if you feel that you aren't being heard, please get your doctor's attention and ask him or her to listen to you. Visiting a doctor can be a traumatic experience and if you don't feel like the doctor is really listening to you, the anxiousness of the moment intensifies.

Also, if you're having a conversation with someone and you catch yourself not listening, let the other person know that you aren't hearing them and then explain why you aren't listening. You don't want to do that? Why not? What's wrong with being upfront with someone about this issue? Seems to me that if you're willing to pay attention to yourself as a conversation partner, the person to whom you're talking will honor your moment of truth with them, and you might be able to continue the conversation in a more balanced fashion.

Finally, the **INTENSITY OF YOUR EMOTIONS** often compromises how you communicate. Being calm, cool, and collected in the midst of emotional turmoil is difficult at best. What we say in the heat of anger, frustration, or any other strong emotion is colored by the intensity of those emotions. Is that a bad thing? Not necessarily, but you need to factor in the emotions and weigh their strength against the clarity of your communication.

The bottom line in all of this talk about communication is that you really need to think about what you want to accomplish when you communicate with someone. That's the key. If your intent is to change someone else's mind about something, forget it. The only person you can change is you. You can be persuasive and passionate, but the best you'll be able to accomplish is to express your thoughts and emotions. If your intent is to validate someone else's thoughts, or you want someone to validate yours, that's okay as long as you know what you want to accomplish when you have this kind of conversation. For every thought and the action that follows it there should be a goal. Communicating is like anything else in life: think about what you want to happen and then figure out how you can transform goals and thoughts into action. Remember though, this only works for you. You can't make things happen for other people. Your choices in communication are there just as they are in every other aspect of being human. Just know that you can only influence your own outcome.

One way to avoid miscommunication is to know what roles various people play in your life and be discriminating about who you talk to about what. If you need an ego boost, talk with the person or people in your life you know will offer that to you. You know who they are. If you need to make a decision and you really haven't made up your mind, find the person in your life whom you know to be the most objective and who will listen to you, help you weigh the options, and then mirror the choices for you. If you want to talk about football you wouldn't seek out someone who knows nothing about the game would you? On the other hand, if you want to "show off" you might talk to someone who knows less about the game than you do. What you want to accomplish in the conversation is the key here.

You might consider communicating like your animal friend does. Use your intuition and don't intellectualize. You always know where you stand with a dog. Dogs are quite clear about their needs and how they feel about almost everything. They don't analyze, judge, or have hidden agendas. What you see is what you get when you have a relationship with a dog. They don't use words, and I think that's a good thing because words get us in trouble sometimes. I know that part of being human involves using words, but what if you could feel, on an intuitive level, what you want to say, and then let your intuition guide your vocabulary? If you're able to do this, all of the considerations I've talked about in the previous paragraphs wouldn't be necessary at all. No need for hidden agendas, no need for posturing and ego dominated conversations, and no need to function as a "yes person." No need for any of the stumbling blocks we place in our own way.

One last aspect of communicating involves body language. There are many books available on this topic, so I won't belabor the point except to say that your body is often an excellent mirror of what you're really trying to say when you communicate. Since your body orchestra is responding to the inner conductor, it might not be a bad idea to be aware of the message your body is sending because your body language often contradicts the words you're using, or if you're listening to someone else, the words they're saying. Unless you're having a conversation out in the middle of a blizzard and you're wrapping your arms around yourself to keep warm, this posture when used in listening generally indicates a closed attitude toward what is being said. If you're telling someone that you're happy and yet you're not smiling, something's off about what you're really feeling. If you tell someone that you feel close to him, but you're standing on the other side of the room and aren't making any move toward the other person, what are you really saying? I know the cliché "actions speak louder than words" is over-used, but there really is some truth to the statement if you think about it, whether you're considering body language or actions that follow speech. If you're not walking your talk, then you haven't decided what your talk is all about.

Do you like the phrase "walking your talk"? Here's an example to illustrate what I mean when I say that it's important to walk your talk: In the first paragraph of the next chapter I mention my friend Nancy within the context of the opening paragraph about relationships. Nancy is the person I think of most often when I think about someone who walked her talk. Nancy was a teacher who was respected and loved by her students because they believed what she told them. Why did they believe her? They believed her because she walked her talk. Regardless of the occasion or situation—teaching history in the classroom, attending a student function, having dinner in a restaurant, or making a speech in front of the school board, Nancy's students—and everyone who knew her—understood that she was the real deal. Everyone who was acquainted with Nancy always knew where they stood with her. Her communication with people was always clear, genuine and consistent. When I was counseling students about walking their talk and I knew they didn't get what I was saying I often sent them to visit with Nancy if they hadn't already met her. She taught by example, rather than just using words.

The mixed messages we send often relate to our confusion and ambivalence about our relationships with people, and that needs to be the next chapter because dealing with other people can be a major source of difficulty, not only in terms of communication, but also with regard to functioning as a successful human.

Chapter 5

RELATIONSHIPS

Pay attention. Be fully present.

I once conducted a memorial service for a friend who had gone on to her next expression of spirit, and as I looked at the people who had come to remember Nancy I was struck by how many different relationships were represented by those in attendance. I saw: husband, children, mother, brother, aunt, uncle, students, colleagues, casual acquaintances, friends, very close friends, hospice caregivers, hospital personnel, and various professional associates. Isn't it wonderful that one person can have so many different relationships? That works for you too. Let's talk about it.

Consider yourself to be a precious cut gem. How about a diamond? Now, think about what happens when you hold a diamond up to the light: As you turn the stone, the facets of the diamond change color depending on light exposure. Every facet may appear to be a different color, or even a different shape, but all of the facets are equally important parts of the diamond. The diamond doesn't exist without the facets, and the facets of the gem don't exist without the stone. We're a bit like many faceted gems; we show different sides of ourselves depending on our relationships with other people, but there's no "real" us buried within the gem.

When you were a kid (or even an adult) you may have said, "You don't really know me" to someone, or perhaps many people. What does that statement mean? It could mean that you showed people only what you wanted them to see. Or, the comment might mean that people only saw in you just what they wanted to see. Perhaps both statements are true. Who we are is often complicated . . . for many reasons.

We can't help but be who we are. No one else has taken up residence in our bodies. Each of us is alive and well inside our suit of armor. Being possessed by a demon—or the spirit of Elvis—are intriguing thoughts, but they're without substance. There's no room for anyone else inside of our bodies and minds. Sometimes there's barely enough room for us, particularly when the "us" encompasses everyone we have ever been or will be. Hold that thought; I'll talk more about "all" of us in the chapter about time.

So, what is it then that makes our relationships with others so difficult? I think several factors contribute to the difficulties we often encounter when we relate to people:

how much we're willing to show and tell, filter systems, not recognizing the relationship for what it is, expectations and assumptions, value judgments, emotional responses, what you need from the relationship, ego, control issues, communication, trust, honesty, responsibility, and finally self-awareness. I know that's a long list, but I have a feeling this is going to be a long chapter because there are many important concepts to consider. Let's take each one and explore the possibilities.

Ever been in an elevator with just one or two other people? Did you smile and say hello, or did you try to avoid eye contact and remain quiet? When you get home from work do you use your garage door opener to open the door before you get to it so you can drive in, shut the door and go into the house without greeting your neighbor who's out mowing his lawn? What's up with this kind of awkward avoidance? This kind of behavior is an aspect of **HOW MUCH YOU'RE WILLING TO SHOW AND TELL**, but on the surface this kind of avoidance really doesn't make much sense. Even if you're tired and don't feel up to any kind of prolonged contact, a smile doesn't take much energy does it? You don't have to tell your life story to the people in the elevator, nor do you have to spend time discussing your personal life with your neighbor. A simple acknowledgment of another person's presence is a way to connect, that's all. There's no need to insulate yourself from connecting with other people. Is there fear involved for you if you indulge in the above mentioned avoidance behaviors? If so, what are you afraid will happen if you smile and greet someone? Perhaps you think that a smile and greeting offer encouragement for further conversation, and you're not willing to go there, for whatever reason. Perhaps you're afraid if you smile at someone they won't smile back. So what if they don't return your smile . . . but I'll bet they will.

When I was teaching psychology I often had my students observe human behavior by performing various social "experiments," and one of my favorites, because it was so simple, was to ask them to smile at everyone they met during the course of one day and keep track of how many people didn't smile back at them. Many of my students thought there was no way that everyone who got a glimpse of their teeth would smile back at them, and they often made predictions about how many non-smiles they'd receive during a day. When they reported back to class all of them were blown away by the fact that everyone they met smiled back at them. Everyone. When I asked my skeptics how they felt about receiving smiles from so many people they all said that they liked being smiled at, and at the end of the day they felt really good. You get the point.

You don't always have to be willing to show and tell very much if you prefer not to, but some kind of connecting with other people—regardless of the situation—is a good thing, and the connection won't lead to more than you're willing to deal with if you don't want it to do so. You're in charge of you, remember? You can show as much or as little of yourself to others as you choose. Just be clear about why you're not willing to make a connection if you're reluctant to do so. You also might want to remind yourself that you decided to come here to experience life on earth, in a body, *and* to interact with others in some way. That interaction is part of being human.

How much we're willing to play Show and Tell with other people can become convoluted because there's often a manipulative aspect to this relationship issue. My mother, for example, was a very manipulative person, and what she showed and told other people about herself often depended on what she wanted from them. I was a constant source of annoyance to her because I refused to be manipulated and would often cut to the chase and just ask her what it was that she wanted. (An aside here about manipulative behavior that needs to be mentioned is that you can't manipulate someone unless they're willing to be manipulated. It's just like so many other topics I've talked about already, in that you don't do or say something to other people and receive an automatic response without their creating and owning that response.) Okay, moving on. My mother didn't need to be manipulative; she was perfectly capable of asking for what she wanted and needed, but the image she cultivated and presented to other people required that she be in control of how other people responded to her. Communication between people doesn't work that way, of course, but she didn't accept that concept. She deluded herself into thinking that how others responded to her was dependent on how well she manipulated them. She did have many people in her life who were willing to be manipulated, for their own reasons, and so she happily continued with this approach for as long as I knew and loved her. She also had a certain aspect of self-loathing to her personality, and she often sabotaged her relationships with people by showing a less than attractive aspect of herself knowing that others would be repelled by the negative trait. There was often a test she conducted that went something like, "Just how much can I push this person before they reject me?" When someone did rebuff her, she was often secretly pleased because that rejection reinforced her negative feelings about herself. Complicated isn't it?

Manipulation isn't the only problem with regard to how much you're willing to show and tell about yourself to others. Often, the how much aspect is a case of appropriateness and comfortableness in terms of personal contact. When I was teaching high school I talked with the football coach about football, about my students who played on the team, and in general our conversations were appropriate to common interests. I didn't ask him how he was getting along with his wife; I didn't talk with him about a particularly unpleasant conversation I'd had with a parent, nor did I tell him what I had dreamed the night before. Mutually, without any discussion, we established certain parameters in our relationship that worked for both of us. No, the guidelines had nothing to do with the fact that he was the football coach and I was, at the time, an English teacher. Several years later another football coach appeared on the scene, and I had a completely different relationship with him. In addition to our conversations about football, we did talk about his wife; I did share conversations I'd had with other people, and we did talk about dreams. What explains the difference in approaches? I could, and think I will, cut to the chase and just say that I liked the second guy better than I did the first, and both of them would probably have expressed similar opinions about me.

Can our boundaries really be that simple? Does what you show and tell about yourself really depend on how much you like the person to whom you're talking? Sure, why not? I've found myself talking openly to people I've just met simply because I like them, and I sense that they like me. We all have a kind of internal radar system that tunes in (or out) to people. When I don't connect with someone my conversation with that person reflects that lack of connection. It's not really even a judgment about them; it's just that we don't click. That lack of clicking doesn't have to be a problem, but rather just establishes the boundaries, that's all.

There's one more step involved in the show and tell aspect of relationships and that's the "walk your talk" piece. I talked about this idea in the previous chapter, but I think that it's important enough to mention again. Once you decide how much you're willing to show and tell to the various people in your life, then you need to go one step further and be sure that you bring something to the party. Act on your decisions. Contribute. Walk your talk. Show people by your actions that you are who you say you are. Inconsistencies between what you say and what you do create confusion, and it's important that your relationships with people are as clearly defined as possible.

One last comment about the show and tell topic: it helps to be aware of why you do or don't show certain aspects of who you are to certain people. You don't necessarily have to do anything about what you show and tell unless you discover that there are inconsistencies involved that create problems for you; just be aware of the connection—or lack of it—and the boundaries you're establishing with people.

Our **FILTER SYSTEMS** can also present problems in our relationships with other people. When I was talking about communication I said that we don't always hear what's being said, and other people don't always hear what we're saying. Is this filtering idea just a matter of communication then? No, I think not. When we're born we have a tape recorder in our heads that runs continuously throughout our lives. The recorder never shuts off. Every conversation, emotion, connection you've ever had, is all there. For obvious reasons of maintaining our sanity and perspective, we don't access all of that information all the time, but it's all there constantly influencing our perception of the world. We play those tapes back now and then just to reinforce the experiences that surrounded them.

What this little tidbit of information means with regard to relationships is that sometimes when we're talking with someone what they say is filtered, and then we hear a portion of an old tape. For example, I could say to you, "Do you like living where you live?" An innocent question on my part, asked out of curiosity and an interest in getting to know you. You hear the question, the words get filtered, and then an old tape of your father saying to you, "How can you live in this place?" surfaces, and you respond by saying, "What's wrong with where I live?" Or perhaps you don't respond that openly, but you feel defensive. I pick up on your defensiveness and wonder what's going on. Do you see what's happening here? Your relationships, whatever they are, are compromised by your filer system, which you've programmed to access old tapes. Sometimes a question is just a question. There isn't always a hidden agenda. The key here is that if you find yourself having some kind of intense emotional response to a question someone has asked you, you might want to check your filter system and see if it needs cleaning.

Another road hazard that often becomes visible in relationships has to do with **NOT RECOGNIZING THE RELATIONSHIP FOR WHAT IT IS.** Your idea of what a particular relationship is all about may be different than the idea of the person with whom you're interacting. If you're traveling on a different wave length than someone else in terms of how you see your relationship the wheels could fall off any time. Think about a time when your relationship with someone fell apart because you wanted to be friends and the other person wanted you to be his or her lover. Or vice versa. Oops . . .

When I was in high school my senior English teacher was a formidable woman named Gerda Boss. I think she's the only high school teacher whose name I remember. Anyhow, she was very tall, thin, plain in appearance, and her teeth clicked when she talked. She was very strict, incredibly bright, and I loved her class because she always challenged us to read and appreciate English literature. She was also the advisor of the drama program; in retrospect I think this was a rather unlikely interest for her because she was quite reserved and rarely smiled. Perhaps she lived vicariously through the productions she directed. Who knows? At any rate, I was one of those high school students who was involved in a variety of activities ranging from playing sports to being in the drama program. I wasn't a very good actress because I was too busy directing (in my mind) to pay attention to the part I was playing, but I joined the club because Miss Boss was the advisor. I found myself wanting to be wherever she was, never recognizing that I was indulging myself in an absurd adolescent obsession that really had no substance and would never, in a million years, be reciprocated on any level. This fixation wasn't a crush in a sexual sense, but was more of a wanting to function on the same intellectual level that she did. Oh, I knew that she liked and respected me because I was a good student, but I'm sure, in retrospect, that her thoughts about me didn't extend beyond how she viewed me as a student. One night she gave me a ride home after play practice, and for some reason I felt compelled to tell her how wonderful I thought she was. I think I went on and on (fortunately, I don't really remember what I said) and after she listened politely she told me that my energies could be better spent studying literature instead of fixating on her. She reminded me that she was my teacher, not my colleague; in short, she cut me off at the pass. Naturally, I was crushed because I had somehow fantasized that she and I could talk as equals and perhaps go off into the sunset together (in hindsight a rather ludicrous thought) and be co-teachers in some sort of weird parallel universe. Or something. I really blew it because our relationship was never the same after that awkward conversation. Because I was young, I didn't recognize the relationship for what it was, and instead of really thinking about how we did relate to one another, I just ignored reality and obsessed about my fantasy relationship with her.

You're probably thinking that the above example is a common one for teenagers, but I think as adults we often do the same thing. We don't pick up the cues that someone else is giving us, and instead we just barrel ahead with our own perception of what's going on. This is a good example of how our intuition would serve us well if we'd only use it. Intuitively you know what your relationships with other people are all about. Trust what you feel and save your fantasies for your dreams.

Sometimes our **EXPECTATIONS AND ASSUMPTIONS** about other people really get us into trouble in our relationships. Even though it's perhaps reasonable to expect certain behaviors from people you know fairly well, and to also assume that certain things might be true about your interaction with someone with whom you share a close relationship, I know you've found on occasion that this is a very slippery slope. Before you know what's happened you're sliding down the slope on your butt wondering where and why you lost your footing.

Here's the deal: people like to be treated with respect, and they don't like to be taken for granted. This is true for you, right? As part of this same scenario, you also don't like other people to assume that certain things are true about you when they don't have enough information to make that assumption. What's that old cliché about the word "assume"? Something about making an ass out of you and me, I think.

In order to understand how expectations and assumptions cause trouble in relationships all you have to do is put yourself in the equation . . . on the receiving end. When someone had expectations about you that weren't true, how did you feel? When someone made an assumption about you that wasn't accurate, how did you feel? Okay, so you get that this is not a productive way of relating to people, but why then do we expect and assume?

Sometimes I think it's a matter of feeling so comfortable with someone you forget that the person still gets to choose how they're going to interact with you. Relationships don't function successfully on automatic pilot, and you don't get to expect certain things from people all the time. Allow room for choice and use your intuitive radar to tell you whether you can expect something or nothing. Just because you've had pizza and sex with your partner on Sunday night for the past six months doesn't mean that you should automatically pick up a pizza on your way home and then expect to have sex later in the evening. Asking what people want lets them know that you consider their choices to be important and are willing to honor them. Simple, really.

Another aspect of expectations and assumptions that you might want to consider is the stagnation factor. Expecting and assuming can become habitual, and it's often just easier to have pizza and sex on Sunday even if you really feel like eating chicken and just want to go to sleep when you hit the bed. Abdication rears its head in this arena too. Be careful. Being fully present is important and honoring your choices is even more important.

VALUE JUDGMENTS are also a biggie in the relationship sabotage arsenal. Judging other people because of their values doesn't ever do much to encourage any kind of productive relationship. I know that you, as I do, have very strong ideas and opinions on certain subjects. We all get to believe as we choose and think what we like about any topic, but I don't get to judge other people because of their values if I want a relationship with them. Having said that, I do know that I do judge other people on occasion. If I know, for example, that a person is a hunter who kills animals for sport, there's no way I can have a relationship with this person. I don't even choose to engage in any kind of conversation with hunters because imposing my beliefs on someone who obviously thinks very differently than I do is an exercise in futility. The imposition factor is where we get in trouble with value judgments and relationships, I think.

There's something very important to be said about allowing other people to think and believe as they choose without imposing our values on them, or judging them because of their values and then expecting to have a successful relationship with them. Sometimes you just have to recognize incompatibility issues and walk away. Trying to have a successful relationship with someone whose values are diametrically opposed to yours just doesn't work. Oh sure, you could indulge in an intellectual discussion with them and perhaps still maintain your cool, but try to go beyond the academic and you're in trouble.

I once saw an episode of Oprah in which Oprah was talking with a white man who used the word "nigger" quite freely. The man insisted that he used the word generically to describe a certain type of behavior by people of all colors, and Oprah told him that he needed to check his reality barometer (my phrase, not hers) because the use of the word was not generic at all and was only used to describe black people. The conversation was calm, rational and polite. Oprah had no relationship with this man, other than the fact that he was a guest on her show, and after each of them had made their points she went on to introduce her next guest. Information presented, discussed, end of story.

I'm not suggesting that you don't get to express your opinion and present your values, but please don't delude yourself into thinking that you're going to change someone else's mind, or that you can have a successful relationship with someone whose values are ones you judge in a negative way. Or vice versa. It's the negative aspect of value judgments that's the key here. Certainly you can, and probably do, have successful relationships with people whose values differ from yours. The difference in values isn't the problem. The problem exists when you judge someone else's values in a negative way and that judgment impacts your interaction with this person. It's okay not to have relationships with people who have values that you judge negatively; being human doesn't mean that you have to relate to everyone.

Another aspect of relationships that proves to be difficult for many people involves **EMOTIONAL RESPONSES.** If you find yourself having a very strong—either positive or negative—emotional response to something that someone has said or done you might want to look at what's going on with you in terms of why you responded as you did. You'll notice that I said what's going on with you, not the other person. As I've said before, people get to be who they are and the only thing you have any control over is how you respond.

Sometimes we respond emotionally as we do to certain people because it's a bit like looking in the mirror. The people we like are often very much like us. The people we don't like are also often very much like us. Think about what pushes your emotional response buttons. The people to whom we react in a very strong emotional way touch us in some way that's very significant. When you give this topic some thought it's important to be honest with yourself about the why behind your response. Verbalizing what you've come up with in your reflections isn't always necessary, but it is necessary to acknowledge to yourself why you respond as you do. Because I've already talked about how important my relationship is with dogs, you shouldn't be surprised that I respond very positively to people who share that connection. I'm never surprised either when I meet someone who loves and respects dogs that I have a strong positive emotional response to them.

On the other hand, I tend to be a "the best way to get it done is to do it yourself" kind of person, and when I meet someone who exhibits this same tendency I often have a negative response to him or her. Why? I'm seeing this often unwelcome control freak trait mirrored in someone else, and I recognize immediately that this person is acting just like me, and not in a flattering way.

Here's a specific example of what I've just talked about: When I was directing theater (Yes, I finally did as an adult what I did in my head as a kid) I always had a stage manager who was responsible for making sure the props were in place before a performance. On one particular occasion I went early to the theater, as I always did, and was busy making sure that the props were all in place. My stage manager came in and asked what I was doing. When I told her she laughed and said, "That's my job, you know. Don't you trust me to do my job the way you taught me? You can check after I've placed the props, but don't do my job for me." My stage manager was sixteen and I was twenty-five at the time. Like I said before, age isn't necessarily a determiner of wisdom. She was right; I needed to let her do the job I had assigned her. By doing the job myself I wasn't allowing her to learn. She was a very good mirror.

Another thing to consider is **WHAT YOU NEED FROM YOUR RELATIONSHIPS** with people. We all need something from other people, and matching the need with the person is the key to having a successful relationship. As I've mentioned before, if you need an ego boost, find the person who will give that to you. If you need to laugh, contact the person you can laugh with and have fun. If you need to have a serious conversation about your hopes and dreams, find the person in your life that you can talk with about those topics. You know who these people are, and acknowledging your needs and then acting on them is a healthy and very clear way of relating to people. Of course, doing this requires that you be clear about what you need from people and then being willing to follow through on that thought. You can do that. Sometimes a very simple approach works really well. Consider the following example:

I once knew a man who was ill and couldn't get out much. He loved to play checkers and really wanted to have someone in his life who liked to play checkers. Unfortunately, he didn't know anyone who liked to play as much as he did. So, because he was a man who believed in following through on his needs, he put a sign up in his front yard that said: "Wanted: Checkers Player. Inquire Within." One day a young boy knocked at the door and said that he played checkers. That was the beginning of a wonderful relationship between my friend Marty and his new friend, Steve. Steve came by after school several days a week and he and Marty played checkers. There wasn't really anything more to the relationship than checkers, but this common interest in the game was enough for both of them because they didn't need anything else from each other.

I've mentioned **EGO** before when I was talking about communication, and how you feel about yourself deserves another comment here with regard to relationships. Your sense of self has a great deal to do with how you relate to other people. If you're confident and self-assured, you're liable to relate to people in a very clear way without any hidden agendas or booby traps. You won't need to cultivate relationships with people to boost your ego, or if you tend to be masochistic, to re-enforce your fragile sense of self-worth. This concept goes back to what you need from people and your awareness of those needs. You're in charge of your own ego; other people can't make you feel better about yourself. Acknowledging how you feel about yourself and then looking at your various relationships with people is a good idea because what you come up with will tell you why your relationships are working and why they aren't.

My friend Herb is very insecure about himself. He has a very difficult time making decisions because he's always afraid that he'll make the "wrong" decision, and he often relates to people in a tentative manner. He's also found, in moments of clarity, that many people are turned off by his insecurities. Intellectually he knows that he's constantly seeking approval from other people, and he also knows this approach can be very annoying. He does have people in his life who like to have him consult them about every little thing, but he has a hard time not approaching everyone in the same way that he relates to those people who enjoy being his sounding board. Herb and I have known each other for a very long time, and he knows when he comes to me and asks me to tell him what to do that I won't answer him in the way he wants me to respond. He knows this and yet he still does it. I'm acquainted with most of Herb's friends, and so when he comes to me with one of his "Tell me what to do" questions, I just say, "You know I'm not going to do that. You need to ask Jessica." His response is invariably the same each time. He smiles and says, "Okay. I'll do that." If my approach sounds insensitive to you please remember that Herb gets to be who he is, and it's not my role in his life to enforce change on him if he chooses not to change, nor is it my place to judge him because of his insecurities. He's a great guy; we have many interests in common, and so I enjoy his friendship on the level that works for both of us. Do I wish he weren't so insecure? Sure, but I have no control over how he feels about himself. If, someday, he chooses to have the "I need to change how I relate to people and I need your help" conversation, then we'll have a different kind of interaction.

Another facet of the ego issue in terms of relationships has to do with needing to be "right" all the time to preserve a perception of yourself as being someone who is an authority on everything. This tactic doesn't endear you to people, but rather suggests to people that you're a pain in the ass rather than a friend or acquaintance. Being mistaken about something shouldn't destroy your ego. If being wrong about something bothers you that much you might want to look inside rather than using external events to mold your personality. It's all about learning, remember?

CONTROL ISSUES also often get in the way of successful relationships. I've already touched on the subject briefly when I was talking about my mother, but perhaps a few additional comments might also be helpful. When you attempt to mold your relationship with someone else by trying to control him or her, you're really courting disaster.

Once again, the only person you have any control over is you. You can control how you respond to other people but not how they respond to you. I once saw a book title that read *What You Think of Me is None of My Business*, and I've always liked the thought behind the title. Of course, we care about what other people think of us, but we can't control their thoughts and feelings. Just be who you are and allow people to respond to you as they will. They're going to do that anyway, so you may as well relax and just be as clear as you can be with people. I'm not suggesting that this concept gives you permission to be a jerk, or to be unkind to people, because there is, after all, the matter of respect for others; that's an important consideration. You know what I mean.

COMMUNICATION issues also play a huge part in your relationships with other people. I've devoted a whole chapter to the topic of communication, so not much else needs to be said at this point except to remind you that how you communicate with people makes all the difference between successful and unsuccessful relationships. Clear communication is the glue that holds your healthy relationships together.

Another quality that I think of as glue—actually more like cement—in relationships is **TRUST**. If you don't trust the people in your life with whom you have relationships you're just going through the motions and nothing very real is happening in your interactions. How and why you trust other people could be, and often is, a topic deserving of a whole book in itself, but there are a few comments that might be relevant in this context. Here again, as I've said before, you draw to yourself. If you're a trustworthy person then you'll draw others who can be trusted to you. It's really that simple. If you tend not to trust people and find yourself questioning their motives you might want to look in the mirror. If you view the people with whom you interact as extensions of yourself there's no need to be concerned about trust, unless you don't trust yourself. Trust is really just a matter of always being willing to look for the good in people. Why wouldn't you? Why would you spend time and energy second-guessing the motives of other people? Again, look to yourself. There's so much about relationships that depends on your willingness to look in the mirror. Keep one handy so you don't forget to do that. Trust what you see.

HONESTY is another factor that needs to be mentioned with regard to relationships. We aren't always honest with other people, and we aren't always honest with ourselves. Let's take honesty with other people first.

Here again our concern for the feelings of others comes into play as an issue. It's not always safe to assume that people want you to be honest with them. On the other hand, it's also not safe to assume that they don't either. How can you tell? Use your intuition. Don't get caught in the trap of not wanting to hurt someone else's feelings by being honest with them. Remember what I said about this in an earlier chapter: You can't hurt someone else's feelings. They do that all by themselves. You do, I think, have to weigh how important it is to be honest with someone. Think about the topic of conversation and evaluate the significance of your response in the vast scheme of things. For example, if someone asks you if you like the shirt they're wearing and you absolutely hate it, how important is it for you to tell them that you wouldn't wear that shirt if someone gave it to you? Not very I think, but if you're inclined to be a purist in these kinds of conversations, go ahead and tell them the shirt is awful, at least from your perspective. This is one of those hidden agenda questions anyway because in most cases the person asking is looking for a compliment, and really all you have to decide is if you feel like being complimentary. You could also do a fast shuffle and side step the whole honesty issue and tell them that the shirt looks great on them. That way you've told them what they probably want to hear without perjuring yourself.

I know that the above example is pretty superficial, so let's move on to a more significant aspect of the same issue.

Being honest with people *is* important on many levels, particularly if you have a close relationship with someone. Not telling the important people in your life the truth about how you feel about them or how you feel about something they've said or done serves no useful purpose. In fact, this kind of avoidance perpetuates a lack of commitment to the relationship. The health of the relationship suffers if you aren't honest. If you have strong feelings about something a friend, or perhaps your spouse has done or said it's good to express those feelings right away. If you don't, other similar situations will occur and one day you'll find yourself having what I call an "everything out of the closet" conversation in which you list everything that has bothered you about this person for the past six months. Deal with these concerns as they occur and don't hoard them. Having said that, I think it's also important to recognize that you don't get to impose your honest opinions if they haven't been asked for unless there's an issue of comfortableness involved. It's also a question of timing and how you phrase your thoughts and feelings. There's a difference between being honest and being too blunt and even unkind in how you express your opinions. You know the difference; just use your common sense in how you approach this issue.

The other aspect of honesty has to do with the fact that we aren't always honest with ourselves. Are you someone who should be wearing a tee shirt that says, "Denial Ain't Just A River in Egypt"? If you're going to have healthy and successful relationships with people you need to be honest with yourself before you can even hope to be honest with other people. That old cliché about not being able to love someone else until you love yourself applies here too, I think. Mostly this business about not being honest with yourself comes up when someone says or does something about which you have a strong reaction, as I've mentioned earlier. If your buttons get pushed consistently by the same issues you might want to take a look at the why behind your responses. In many cases if you do this you'll find that looking in the mirror of someone else's behavior and thoughts brings up the question of your own behavior and thoughts. If you're honest with yourself about why you feel as you do it's much easier to understand why you respond as you do.

I have someone in my life who recently had an unsettling experience with her brother. They apparently started out having an ordinary kind of conversation that ended up in a shouting match. My friend left the room in a huff and later called me to talk about what had happened. Without going into detail about their conversation I'll just say that what was going on was simply evidence of the fact that my friend Janet really doesn't like her brother. When I made this observation to her, Janet was horrified that I would suggest such a thing. "What do you mean I don't like him? He's my brother." So? One of the illusions we perpetuate in our relationships with family members is that just because we're related to someone we automatically like and love them. We don't automatically have feelings about anyone, regardless of what our relationship is with them. In our society we expect three, four, or however many people to live peacefully together in the same house just because they're related to each other, but any relationship takes work, and we don't automatically always love or like our relatives. In the case of Janet and her brother she actually knew that she didn't like him, but she stuffed those feelings because she thought because he was her brother she was supposed to like him. She wasn't being honest with herself about how she felt about him because she got caught up in the "shoulds" of family dynamics. After our conversation she did finally admit that she doesn't like him. It'll be interesting to see if their relationship changes because of that self-realization.

RESPONSIBILITY is another factor that comes into play when considering relationships. We're only responsible for ourselves, but this is an intricate issue, especially if we're talking about honoring our responsibilities in terms of the commitments we make to other people. If things run amok in your relationship with your partner or spouse, for example, blaming him or her for whatever is going on without considering your part in the equation is irresponsible and shows a lack of commitment to the relationship.

In another context, but with the same principle in mind, as a teacher I always felt I was responsible for what I taught and my students were responsible for what they learned. We each brought our part of the bargain to the table, and hopefully learning occurred—for all of us—because of how I taught and how they learned. Education was a partnership in which I loved to participate because teaching and learning were exciting and challenging. I couldn't possibly be responsible for what my students learned, any more than they could be responsible for what I taught. My job was to do my best to teach in a way that would motivate them to learn, but if they decided not to learn, then that was their choice. Readiness often made a huge difference in terms of when learning occurred.

I once taught a group of seniors who had to pass my class in order to graduate from high school. What I taught in terms of reading, writing and grammar were topics that had been presented to them for many years, but they'd chosen not to learn. Not until these seniors were faced with the possibility of not graduating did learning the material become important to them. For the first time in twelve years they became responsible students because they were ready and willing to learn. Being held accountable throughout <u>all</u> of the stages of education was always one of my soap box topics because I saw all too often that until a real bottom line was presented students just blew off what was taught to them . . . but I digress.

Be responsible when you're dealing with other people. Acknowledge that you play a part in the relationship—whatever that part is—and do your part in owning up to your share of glory . . . or dysfunction. You can't be responsible for other people, but you can be responsible in dealing with them.

Finally, (this really is a long chapter) your **SELF-AWARE-NESS** is a major contributor to the success of your relationships. I've mentioned this topic briefly, but now it's time to put the bow on the package. All of the other issues in this chapter really come down to your sense of self and how that very important aspect of who you are affects your relationships with other people. In order to assess how this works, you need to look inside. Once again, external events don't determine your sense of self. It's how you respond to the events and people in your life that tell you about who you are.

How then do you become aware of who you are and why you relate to people as you do? Pay attention. Be fully present. Participate in your life; it's not a spectator sport. If things are going well and you're enjoying your relationships with the various people in your life, celebrate those connections and keep on doing what you're doing. If, on the other hand, there are problems in any of the areas I've discussed in this chapter, stop long enough to think about the why behind the problem and fix your part of the equation.

How do you fix your part? You look at the topics we've discussed, see which ones fit your particular situation, understand how whatever it is impacts your relationships, and don't do it anymore. I know that sounds simplistic and you'll be tempted to bring out childhood experiences, the other person's issues, and whatever else you can think of as reasons why you can't change your behavior, but that kind of deflecting mentality is a cop out. If something is broken you either fix it or throw it away. In either case, you don't try to use a broken whatever over and over again and expect different results. Look for the patterns (I'll talk more about that in the next chapter) in your relationships with people, and if you see the same kind of unsettling thing happening over and over again, it might be time for you to look at what goes wrong each time. I guarantee that you'll see a pattern, and then it'll be up to you to decide whether or not you choose to break the pattern and make different choices about how you relate to other people. For those of you who don't like change and would rather continue a habitually unsuccessful pattern in your relationships with people, this is going to be tough, but the work you do in terms of self-awareness will produce some really significant results if you're willing to look in the mirror. Oh, and when you do that, don't forget to smile.

Chapter 6

Patterns

If the pattern doesn't work, change it.

I've always been fascinated with the patterns that exist in our lives. Even in one lifetime we function in a kind of patterned existence predicated upon our acceptance or rejection of the lessons we've chosen to learn. People who marry several times, for instance, often choose the same type of person to share their lives over and over again, even if the previous marriage failed because of incompatibility issues. People are drawn to each other in a patterned kind of way. The patterns are there, and I think that sometimes our inability to recognize the patterns in our lives impacts our ability to be successful human beings because we perpetuate behavior that isn't productive, and because we haven't noticed the patterns we feel stuck.

Sometimes the pattern becomes a treadmill that seems to keep us moving without progress. This state of being comes from an inability to recognize the choices available to us. To feel as though we're in a rut indicates that control has been relinquished and responsibility is being ignored. We can change the patterns any time we wish to do so, but first we need to recognize that the patterns exist.

I think it's important to understand—on any level—that the patterns in our lives exist, and even more significantly, to understand that we create the patterns. They don't just happen. To develop the ability to reflect, evaluate, (not judge) and then decide if the pattern works in a positive way is a good thing to do. If the pattern doesn't work, change it. Don't say you can't, because you can if you choose to do so. If you feel stuck in a patterned existence that doesn't work for you, then perhaps you might want to look at why you need the pattern. Sometimes patterns, like so many other aspects of our lives, become habitual and comfortable regardless of how effective they are, and habits, as you well know, are often difficult to change because sometimes it's just easier to continue with things as they are and ignore the negative aspects of the pattern. Remember the pizza and sex example from the previous chapter?

Just for fun, think about how you get dressed in the morning. If you're like most people, you probably put your clothes on in exactly the same way every day. Do you put both socks on and then both shoes? Do you put one sock and then one shoe on before you move on to the next foot? Once again, this is a trivial example, but I want you to think in simple terms about patterns before we talk about the big ones. How you get dressed may be a simple matter of efficiency, and the same could be said of many other patterns that exist in your life, but what if efficiency isn't the issue? What if the patterns you create are a matter of avoidance, denial, lack of trust, or any other unsuccessful behavior? The principle is the same whether we're talking about how you get dressed, how you choose friends, how you spend your time, or how comfortable you are in certain situations. We create patterns for reasons.

The patterns we create are often done so without much conscious thought, but there are always reasons behind the choices we make in terms of the patterns in our lives. We aren't always aware of those reasons, but all you have to do is look at whether or not the pattern works for you and ask yourself why it does or doesn't work. It's really very simple, but sometimes we're lazy about making changes in our lives even if those changes will improve our abilities to be successful human beings.

I once counseled a man who was very frustrated by the fact that his relationships with women always ended badly. He said that he wanted to marry, have children, and live happily ever after with one woman. What he said, however, and what he did were two different things. The women he chose and pursued were always unavailable for one reason or another. They were either married already, involved with someone else, emotionally inaccessible, or just plain not interested in him. When I asked him why he thought that he always seemed to choose women who were unavailable he looked at me like I had two heads and was speaking to him in Swahili. He couldn't wrap his head around my question, so I asked him why he was afraid of commitment. (No point in fooling around when you can just cut to the chase.) He didn't like this question any better than the first, but I did have his attention. Long story short, this man, in spite of his fantasy about living happily ever after with one woman, was actually terrified of cultivating this kind of relationship. Why? Because he really wasn't sure he had much to offer a marriage and family, he deliberately chose women who were safe companions so he wouldn't have to deal with his own perceived inadequacies. The problem for him, though, was that he was unhappy and lonely. So, we talked about what would have to happen in order for him to trade his current life for one in which he might be happy. He's still working on it.

We create and choose our patterns in the same way that we do everything else, but it's difficult to see a pattern if you're right in the middle of it. In that sense hindsight is always a terrific learning experience, but often we don't apply what we've learned to the next experience. It's not impossible to recognize a pattern in your life while you're participating in it, but achieving a little distance from yourself to look at how you're functioning is helpful. Are you happy with the choices you've made? Is the pattern a comfortable one? Are you learning anything? If your answer to any of the above questions is no, then some consideration needs to be given to the choices made and the patterns that result from those choices. Nothing is so inflexible that change isn't possible.

As an exercise in awareness, you might look at your activities in a one-day period of time from the moment you get up in the morning until you fall asleep at night. What I'm asking you to do is simply to look at your daily routine. Once you do that, then the next step is to see if there's anything in that routine that doesn't work for you, or that you don't like for whatever reason. If you find something, change that part of the routine and see what happens. Keep at this for a while until you have a routine that feels comfortable and productive. This new feeling won't happen overnight because patterns and routines aren't always easy to change, but if it's important enough to you, you can do it.

Then, expand your view to your relationships with people and look at the patterns that exist in that arena. Once again, if you see a pattern that's negative, not productive, or just not very fulfilling, take steps to effect change in this area too. It's just a matter of making different choices, that's all. Just keep in mind that the only patterns you can change are your own.

Continuing the above thought, consider your general behavior and how you handle change, stress, conflict, or anything you perceive to be negative in your life. When you face change, how do you react? If you feel stressed, how do you respond? If you have a difference of opinion with someone that results in some sort of conflict, how do you handle the situation? I ask these questions because I think if you look at your responses to certain situations you'll find that your behavior follows the same pattern each time. In cases that you might describe as being positive, you'd probably use the word "consistent" to describe your behavior. Consistency isn't a problem if the results are comfortable for you, but if they aren't . . . well, you know what to do.

No doubt you're familiar with the obsessive compulsive personality. Hopefully those words don't describe you, but if they do, your need to do things in exactly the same way every time is a box into which you've put yourself. Patterns can be obsessive too, and as such they provide a nice, safe cocoon in which you can hide. If you take refuge in the patterns in your life you might want to ask yourself why you're afraid to change the pattern. There's that word again: fear. Patterns are safe because we become comfortable with the routine of them whether we're dealing with people, learning experiences, eating habits, how we spend our time, or any aspect of our lives. We all have our comfort zones and sometimes it's very uncomfortable to move out of those safe areas. As I've mentioned before, it's not always necessary to change a pattern in your life, but if you find yourself doing the same things over and over again expecting different results, then it's time to look at the pattern you've created and think about changing it.

I once knew a young man who was a very talented artist. His pen and ink drawings were exquisitely detailed and I loved studying them. My only question for him had to do with the subject matter because all of his drawings were renditions of the same comic book characters. Each drawing was like looking at the same subject over and over again. When I suggested that he might like to study art (he'd had no formal training) so he could learn to expand his subject matter a bit he said, "Why? This is what I do. I don't want to learn how to draw anything else." He was very adamant about his work because he was very comfortable in his zone and didn't want to leave the safety of his success with the comic book characters. He probably would have had a very successful career as a comic book illustrator, but that isn't what he said he wanted to do. He said that he wanted to be the kind of artist whose paintings hung in museums and galleries.

As I write this I'm also thinking about a very talented young woman who had leading roles in many of the productions I directed. She said she wanted to pursue a career in the theater, and because I felt that she had the talent and work ethic to be successful, I arranged for her to audition with a professional theater group. At first she was excited about the opportunity to strut her stuff in front of the pros, but when the time came for her to make the trip to the city for the audition she backed out and wouldn't go. When I asked her why she hadn't chosen to audition she said that in our small town she was a star—a big fish in a small pond—and she was afraid that if she tried to compete with actors in the big city she wouldn't be successful, and she'd rather continue to enjoy her fame in a small town instead of risking failure in the big city.

In both of the above cases the people involved left themselves no room for expansion. They both insisted that they wanted careers in art and acting respectively, but they were unwilling to change the pattern of their actions to accommodate their dreams. Sometimes fantasies are more fun than reality, and if you never try to move beyond your current abilities you may never experience failure, but you also leave yourself no room for success either. It's a bit like not studying for a test, failing it, and then saying, "I could have done well, but I didn't study." Yeah, right. Very safe.

Sometimes the patterns that exist in our lives are not only very comfortable, but they're productive and we function as happy human beings. Hang on to those patterns and use them as a barometer for your evaluation of the ones that don't feel that way. Comparison is a good tool and often leads to some interesting insights.

Insights= Sighting or looking inside. That's where all of the action is. Don't look for external reasons to explain the patterns in your life. Look inside.

Chapter 7

DREAMS

Dreaming allows the essence of who we are to become activated and surface for our consideration and enjoyment.

Dreams? Are you thinking that somehow I've included a chapter that belongs in a different book? Nope. My last words in the previous chapter were "Look inside," remember? Talking about dreams is very relevant. I'll explain.

It seems to me that since being human is difficult for most of us we need all the help we can get to understand our behavior. I've found looking at dreams to be a very effective and often under-rated tool that can offer some really interesting insights about how we function as humans.

I'm a very practical person. For me, information needs to work in some way that's useful. Telling me how my computer is put together isn't helpful to me because I just want to know how to use it. Analyzing Shakespeare's plays by taking the dialogue apart, line by line, drives me crazy.

Too much analysis of any topic is what I call "shredding the rose." Certainly you can gain a detailed view of how a rose is constructed by taking it apart petal by petal, but when you've completed the task of removing each petal you've destroyed the rose and are left with a pile of petals on the floor. Not necessary or productive.

What is necessary, for any kind of analysis, is to be clear about what you want to learn and why you want to learn it. You're reading this book because you want to learn how to be a successful human being and you want to learn this information because . . . well, you supply the reason. I'm about to talk about dreams and how they work for us, and I want you to be able to use this information in a very practical way.

Freud, Jung et al. aren't invited to this discussion; this isn't a chapter that will give you a *Reader's Digest* version of dream symbols; you won't be reading an esoteric commentary about how your spirit guides help you understand your dreams; theories about other cultures and their dreaming isn't included, and there won't be any elaborate instructions about how to remember your dreams. So, what's left?

You'll find what I have to say to be simple, but sometimes the simplest tasks are difficult because as humans we have a tendency to complicate our lives. It's almost as if we feel that something isn't valid unless it's complicated and difficult. Scratch that idea. I won't be shredding the rose here. What I will be doing is giving you some thoughts about dreams that you can put to good use.

We all dream. All the time. Day and night. Dreaming is a necessary aspect of being alive. Whether you find yourself daydreaming while you're sitting in a boring meeting, or dreaming at home while you're asleep in your bed, you dream. Your imagination allows you to create dreams, and these creations are constructed in your subconscious mind. I know that there are many terms I could use to describe that place I'm calling "subconscious," but that word is as good as any.

In your subconscious mind there are no barriers or restrictions. There are no limitations; there's no censorship, or any other kind of conscious contrivance. It's a place of pure imagination uncontaminated by society or anything else. It's the essence of you.

But there's a problem here. We create dreams in our subconscious mind, but then we attempt to analyze them from a conscious mind perspective. That's tough because it's like describing an apple while looking at an orange. Here's an example of what I mean:

When I was in college I wrote quite a bit of poetry. I even kept a paper and pen by the bed because sometimes I had what I thought were brilliant flashes of poems while

I was sleeping and I didn't want to forget them. I trained myself to wake up just enough to jot down ideas so I could look at them in the morning. Well, what happened was that when I was fully awake the fabulous words and images that I'd written down while I was half asleep didn't make any sense at all. Gibberish. For a long time I couldn't figure out what was going on, but then I finally realized that my subconscious images didn't look the same through my conscious eyes. Consciously we place too many limitations and restrictions on ourselves to really get the full flavor of subconscious ideas. They become distilled by conscious thought. Think again about my analogy of apples and oranges. Both are fruit but they're not the same.

This is why dreams are so tricky. They occur in our subconscious mind, yet we try to analyze them using our conscious mind. So, what's the answer? Analyze them using our subconscious? No. There's no room for analysis in the subconscious mind. That place is reserved for intuition, imagination, and feelings. No thoughts. Just pictures. How about dreaming consciously? Then there would be no conflict of interests. That would be ideal of course, but we're too restricted by our own self-imposed limitations to do any kind of real work on a purely conscious level. We're too busy analyzing and judging to get anything really clear.

How about this? What if we just accepted that our

dreams are fueled by our imagination, which lives somewhere in our subconscious mind, and then honored and respected our ability to imagine something that might be important to remember consciously? There doesn't have to be a closed door separating one aspect of your mind from another. If there's a door there, you've created it. You can take that barrier away as easily as you put it there.

Okay. Your dreams are created by your imagination in your subconscious mind. *You* are doing it, by the way. The dreams are yours. No one else is in there creating for you. You're in charge of your dreams just as you are everything else in your life. You can't abdicate responsibility for your dreams by thinking that someone or something is inside your head making you dream. You're dreaming because you need to dream. Why? Just because. Dreaming is part of being alive. The dreaming allows the essence of who we are to become activated and surface for our consideration and enjoyment.

Now the question becomes, why do we dream certain kinds of dreams? I've come up with seven different types of dreams that we create depending on what's going on in our lives. Once you determine which kind of dream you're having, all you have to do is ask yourself two simple questions: How do I feel in the dream, and what's going on in my life that's inspiring my imagination to create the dream? By the time I've finished talking about the different types of dreams I'd be willing to bet that you'll have some light bulbs going off in your head and you'll have figured out what your dreams actually mean. No intricate analysis required. Just a bit of insight.

Let's begin with what I call **PHYSICAL** dreams. For example, you could be dreaming that you're in the middle of the desert. You feel very hot and are having a difficult time breathing. You wake up gasping for air and discover that your electric blanket is turned on to the highest setting and a part of the blanket is covering your face. Your imagination has taken an ordinary physical sensation and created a scenario to match what's going on. I know you've had these kinds of dreams. There are other examples I could give to illustrate the point, but I'm sure you get the idea. Your body requires comfort and when you don't provide it messages are sent to your subconscious mind designed to get your attention. Asking yourself how you feel in the dream and thinking about what's going on in your life to precipitate the dream almost aren't necessary questions in these types of dreams because the answers are pretty obvious.

I'll continue with another fairly easy kind of dream: the **ENTERTAINING** dream. Sometimes our dreaming is a bit like watching television and switching channels from program to program. If you've had a particularly difficult day and haven't allowed yourself any time to play, your imagination will provide play time for you while you're dreaming. These dreams are often funny and nonsensical because that's what you need to experience. The other night I dreamt that I was performing a stand-up comedy routine in a nightclub. People were laughing at my stories and I felt happy and frivolous in the dream. The particular day that I dreamt this dream was a long and difficult one for me, and I don't remember laughing or smiling all day. Too much serious stuff going on. I more than made up for the day in my dream and I woke up smiling. See how therapeutic dreams can be? I obviously needed to laugh and my imagination provided a way for me to do that. Neat, huh?

A third type of dream is the **RE-RUN AND FIX IT** dream. If you're like most people you tend to play back the activities of the day in your head before you fall asleep. It's a way of re-visiting the day and checking with yourself to see how you feel about the events of the day. Here's an example presented to me recently by someone who wanted to talk about her dream:

Sheila had a dream in which she was involved in a conversation with a co-worker. The setting for the dream was a local coffee shop. In the dream she was open to what the co-worker had to say to her and the dream was friendly and comfortable. She felt at ease in the dream. What was going on in her life? On the day that she'd had the dream she and a co-worker had a conversation at work. Sheila was upset with her working partner and handled the issue in an accusatory way, leaving the other person no room to respond. Her dream provided her with an opportunity to re-run the conversation and fix what had caused the wheels to come off during the actual encounter. The key here is that in our subconscious mind we don't judge, and so in Sheila's dream she created an opportunity to have a non-judgmental conversation and still say what she needed to say to her co-worker. The day after she talked with me about the dream she invited her co-worker out for coffee and did a much better job of saying what she wanted to say to her without being judgmental and accusatory. Very productive.

A fourth type of dream is the **HOPE** dream. These are the dreams that reflect what we hope for in our lives. This is the kind of dream my friend Greg has quite often before a football game. In his dream Greg sees himself intercepting a pass in the last minute of the fourth quarter and running the whole length of the field to score a touchdown in front of thousands of screaming fans. He runs effortlessly and seems to float down the field as members of the opposing team try in vain to catch him. His touchdown wins the game for his team and he's carried off the field on the shoulders of his teammates. Greg is 12 years old and hasn't developed his athletic skills quite yet, but his dream is created in his imagination and as such is bigger than life. Why not? The events in the dream tell him what he hopes will happen in his next game. There may not be thousands of fans, but when we get creative with storytelling in our subconscious minds there's no need to limit ourselves.

Most hope dreams are pretty easy to figure out, but sometimes we aren't always honest with ourselves consciously, and a little hope dreaming allows us to know what's really going on. Take Cindy, for example:

Cindy has been dating the same guy all through high school and college. Cindy and Bob are about to graduate from college and they've talked for years about what they'll do after graduation. The plan is for them to get married and work for a couple of years until Cindy becomes pregnant with their first child. Bob will continue to work to support the family while Cindy stays at home to take care of the baby. They've talked about this scenario many times and both of them feel like the plan is written in cement. They seem happy and excited about their future together.

Enter Cindy's dreams. Weeks before graduation Cindy

has the same dream night after night. By the way, when you have dreams that repeat themselves over and over again, your subconscious mind is shouting, "Pay attention! This is important!" In her dream Cindy sees herself in a white uniform working in a hospital setting taking care of sick babies. She feels happy and useful doing this work. After she'd had the same dream without variation for about a week Cindy called me and asked what I thought her dream meant. I listened to what she had to say about the dream and then I asked her how long she'd wanted to be a nurse. Silence.

"Nurse? I don't want to be a nurse. I'm getting married in a couple of months. I have a job lined up in an accountant's office."

Long story short, Cindy has really always wanted to be a nurse, but after she and Bob started playing their ". . . after we get married" tapes she abandoned the idea so she could follow their plan. We talked for a while about the fact that being married and being a nurse didn't have to be mutually exclusive, and she hung up saying that she'd think about our conversation and talk with Bob. Several weeks later Cindy called to tell me that she'd enrolled in a nursing program, and the night after she enrolled she had a different kind of dream for the first time in weeks.

Be clear about your hopes.

Dreams that fall into a fifth category are what I call **FEAR** dreams. Some fear dreams are fairly obvious, like dreaming about snakes if you're afraid of snakes, but sometimes we aren't always consciously aware of our fears and don't take the appropriate action to remove the fears. Here's an example of a fear dream that was very disturbing to Jeff, the dreamer, and he really struggled with the idea behind the dream before he accepted the fact that his subconscious mind was presenting a very important lesson for him to consider.

Jeff dreamt that he was stranded on a deserted island. The setting was idyllic and initially he felt very calm and peaceful there. But after a while he began to feel uneasy because he realized that his chances of being rescued varied from slim to none. His feelings shifted from uneasiness to panic and he woke up screaming. I've already mentioned how Jeff felt in the dream so we don't need to ask that question, but when I asked Jeff what was going on in his life that might have precipitated the dream he drew a blank until we started talking about his social life. Turns out he has none. Jeff works very hard at his job and loves being busy and productive. He says that he has no time to socialize and is very comfortable with his solitary lifestyle. Yeah, right. By the time we'd finished our conversation,

Jeff began to realize that he wasn't as comfortable as he thought he was being a loner. He admitted that at times he feels lonely, but when he has those feelings he just puts in more hours at work and the feeling passes. I suggested to Jeff that he might want to revisit the idea of living his life as a hermit and think about how he would feel if he never really had any kind of personal relationships with other people, particularly with someone who might eventually become his wife. Jeff decided that perhaps living the rest of this life stranded on a desert island of his own creation wouldn't be very fun at all, and the last I heard from him he was actually dating someone and participating in a relationship.

You've already figured out that dreams can be very productive, but there's a sixth type of dream that really illustrates that point: **CREATIVE CONFLICT RESOLUTION** dreaming.

We all handle conflict differently, and resolving conflicts often becomes complicated because consciously we place so many limitations and conditions on these kinds of situations. We can't get out of our own way to resolve issues sometimes, and we seem unable to indulge in any kind of lateral thinking, i.e. looking at a problem from a different (and often off the wall) perspective. Here again, because there are no limitations in what we create subconsciously, our conflict resolution dreams can often be very revealing and quite helpful.

Take Lucy, for example. Lucy doesn't like her mother-in-law at all. The two women don't play well together in any situation, and the tension between them is palpable to anyone who sees them together. Lucy feels that her mother-in-law is controlling, possessive of her son, and unreasonable in her demands for attention. Lucy's husband Rich has abdicated and has a difficult time discussing the situation with either his wife or his mother. Lucy's mother-in-law Doris feels that Lucy is taking advantage of her son and isn't being the kind of wife that he needs. I know all three of these people, but have only talked with Lucy about the tension between her and Doris because of her interest in understanding her dreams. After a particularly nasty encounter with Doris, Lucy dreamt that she and Doris had gone on vacation together. Just the two of them. They traveled to Hawaii and spent a week at a friend's condominium. During the week they spent time on the beach, had dinners out, visited tourist attractions, and in general had a wonderful time. Lucy felt happy and excited in the dream because a part of her knew that what was going on was some kind of momentous occasion. Lucy talked with me about the dream because she couldn't figure out why she would ever have a dream that involved her going on vacation with someone she didn't like. She sputtered and stammered her way through the telling of the dream, all the time saying, "I can't believe I would dream something like this. The dream makes no sense to me. I'd never go on vacation with her."

I asked Lucy how much time she's spent with Doris—just the two of them—and her answer was, you guessed it, none. The two of them have always been in the company of other people, most notably, Rich, and they haven't ever dealt with each other privately at all. I suggested to Lucy that her subconscious mind might be telling her that it was time she and Doris got to know one another as people rather than as adversaries in some bizarre battle for Rich's attention. At first Lucy was reluctant to even entertain the idea of spending time with Doris, but I told her that she didn't have to invite her to go to Hawaii with her, but maybe just take her out for coffee or lunch someday.

It took some convincing for Lucy to agree to try this "really dumb idea" but she eventually did invite Doris out for lunch. In her protests before the lunch Lucy had said to me that she didn't think Doris would accept her invitation, but she was wrong. Doris did agree to have lunch (perhaps because she hoped that Lucy was going to tell her that she and Rich were getting a divorce) and they were both surprised by how well the meeting went. I told Lucy that the event might go more smoothly if they didn't talk about Rich, and if she could find some topics of mutual interest other than her husband she might find that she and Doris could relate to each other as people rather than as feuding relatives. I know you'd like me to tell you that now Lucy and Doris are good friends, but that kind of happy ending only occurs so effortlessly in Disney movies. They do, however, actually like one another and have gone shopping together and have even spent evenings together when Rich was away on business. The tension between the three of them has dissipated, and there's a mutual respect and acceptance that has replaced lack of trust and rejection. The situation is now as Lucy has really always wanted it to be because her own creative imagination came up with something that might make the relationship workable.

Finally, there are dreams that I call, for lack of another word, **PSYCHIC** dreams. I've saved this category for last because I've found that if I have a dream that doesn't seem to fit into any of the above six categories, I might be experiencing a non-traditional kind of connection with someone or something. When I have a dream that defies categorizing I then allow myself to consider the possibility that the dream may be more than just an ordinary dream.

We're all able to pick up information in ways that don't include the usual channels of communication, but our conscious minds are often too filled with chatter for us to be very good at sending or receiving information. When we're asleep and dreaming we're much more receptive, and there are no barriers of any kind to prevent us from tuning in to other people in ways that are much clearer than conscious communication.

Psychic dreams, even though they're often difficult to identify, can sometimes be the most illuminating in terms of providing valuable insights. Because we're more receptive when we're dreaming, our ability to send and receive information through dreams is much more accurate than conscious communication.

Psychic dreams take on many forms, depending on what we need to learn from the dream. In these dreams we can "talk" freely with people or animals who aren't actually physically present, and we can break through any kind of conscious barrier we've created and use our intuition to clarify our feelings. How is this possible? We're just sending and receiving energy, that's all. There's nothing esoteric or supernatural about it. The universe is filled with vibrations floating around on various frequencies; psychic dreaming just affords us the opportunity to tap into these vibrations.

As an example of dreams that fall into this category, I'll use my own experiences with animals. Quite often I dream with dogs. Sometimes this is a conscious effort on my part to connect with a particular dog, but many times I just find myself dreaming with a dog, and in the dream I'm often presented with an important bit of information or insight. I used to dream with my dog friend Cassie quite often because when she was awake she was a very busy being our "wildlife warden" and had little time to communicate other than in the obvious ways, but when she was asleep and dreaming we often connected and I was able to talk with her about how she was, what was going on with her, and listen to what she had to say to me. These dreams are often presented in picture form because animals communicate intuitively and have no need for words, but the pictures are always clear and I generally get what's going on without having to deal with words. One night Cassie and I dreamt together and she told me all about a squirrel that lived on the property. She showed me pictures of her and the squirrel "talking" to each other, and I had a very clear sense of how she felt about the squirrel: she was annoyed with him most of the time because she felt that the squirrel was teasing her. Probably quite true.

Another example of a psychic dream that was actually quite helpful can be seen in a dream my mother had about my father several nights after he'd left his body. In her dream my mother was talking to my father, expressing her anxiety about not being able to find his life insurance papers. My father told her exactly where in the house she would find the insurance policy (somewhere she would never have thought to look) so she immediately got out of bed and found the policy right where he said it would be. The connection between my parents, still strong even after my father's departure, enabled my mother to dream a very practical psychic kind of dream.

The primary focus of our psychic dreams is to allow us to connect and learn. All you have to do is permit yourself to be open enough to send and receive information.

I should also mention that often you'll have a dream that may fit into several of the categories I've talked about, so you need to be willing to consider more than one type of dream when you're thinking about what the dream might mean to you. It's even possible to have a dream that fits into all seven categories.

Consider this short version of what I call a "7 out of 7" dream: My friend Paula dreamt that she was in an elevator traveling to the top of the Empire State Building. When she reached the top she was met by a person who proceeded to interview her for a job. In her dream Paula felt nervous, but she carried on as best she could because she really wanted the job. She did, however, answer several questions in what she felt was a less than eloquent manner, and at one point in the interview she told the person with whom she was talking that she needed a break and proceeded to take a small radio out of her purse. She found a rock and roll station and began to dance. In the middle of the dance Paula's mother appeared and told her to just relax and get back to the interview because the job was hers if she really wanted it.

How did Paula feel in the dream? She experienced a variety of emotional responses: claustrophobia in the elevator (physical), happiness when she was dancing (entertaining), clear-headed when she returned to the interview after her dancing spurt because she knew what to do to turn the interview around (re-run and fix), hopeful that she would get the job during the rest of the interview (hope), panic when she felt that the job might be too much to handle (fear), more settled after a bit of internal dialogue (creative conflict resolution), and reassured when her mother appeared (psychic).

Predictably, in her waking life Paula had just interviewed for a new job in New York. She stayed with a friend during the time she was in New York, but her friend's apartment was very small and she wasn't particularly comfortable there. Paula didn't feel that the interview had gone very well and was sure she wouldn't get the job. The night after the interview she had the dream. When she woke up she knew that she had to see if she could salvage the interview somehow, so she called the person who had interviewed her and asked if she could come in for a second conversation. During the second meeting Paula, who is normally a person with a good sense of humor, allowed her humor to surface and she handled herself with confidence and even went over some of her answers to the questions asked and added clarifying comments. She used her dream, on all seven levels, to get herself hired.

If you've been keeping track, you're probably saying, "Okay, I get the six categories, but what about the psychic aspect of the dream?" Not to worry; it's there. Paula's mother died last year and the dream was Paula's way of connecting with her mother and getting what she needed from her. Whether her mother actually visited her or whether Paula was just connecting with her energy in the dream doesn't really matter.

The key to determining whether your dream fits into more than one category is to check your feelings in the dream and also to leave yourself open to the possible psychic aspect of the dream.

Okay, I've quickly presented my seven types of dreams. Much more could be said about each category, but that would be a whole other book and my intent here is just to offer another way that you can learn about yourself and tune in to what's going on with you. Dreams are always important, even if they're just entertaining. Since you're doing the dreaming you're simply allowing your subconscious to speak to you while you're relaxed and not consciously limiting information.

As an added comment I'd like to say that there are also patterns involved in dreaming, and it would be good to consider this aspect of dreams as well as the various categories. Strong emotional responses in your waking life have a tendency to trigger certain kinds of dreams. I'm not talking about another category of dreams here, but rather dreams that take on a particular style based on what you're feeling. For instance, if you feel stressed, your dreams may have a frustrating, anxious, tense quality to them. If you're feeling trapped in some way, your dreams will take on that same limited feeling. The activities may vary, but the feelings are always the same. If you learn to identify the style of the dream, you may be able to shift your dreaming to a more positive direction without feeling like you're on some kind of treadmill experiencing the same feelings over and over again. Try this: if you're feeling stressed, before you fall asleep tell yourself that you don't need to dream about being stressed, but rather you'd like to dream about ways that you can relieve the stress. You can do this. After all, you're the one in charge of your dreams, and so why not use them to resolve problems rather than to exacerbate them? Being stressed in your waking life and then dreaming about being stressed is no fun.

At this point you may be thinking that all of this is interesting, but if you don't remember your dreams how can they be of value to you in learning how to be a more comfortable human being? Fair question. You can train yourself to remember your dreams, but first you need to acknowledge that there are reasons why you might not remember your dreams. You may not remember your dreams because the conscious and subconscious aspects of your mind aren't talking to one another. Or, you might not buy the concept that there even is a subconscious facet to your mind. Then again, you may be very tuned in to your inner self and what you dream becomes part of your consciousness and you don't necessarily need to remember dreaming because you'll act on what you dream without any conscious memory. Maybe you don't want to remember your dreams because you think that what is revealed in your dreaming will be somehow threatening to you. Perhaps you'd rather think about dreams as being imaginative aberrations caused by eating strange combinations of foods rather than thinking about what a dream might mean on a level not related to food. In any case, there are reasons why you don't remember your dreams.

Now, if you'd like to remember your dreams so you can learn from them, here's what you do: First, allow yourself to be open to the idea that dreams are important; then, before you fall asleep tell yourself that you're going to remember at least one dream. Don't set yourself up for failure by saying that you're going to remember all of your dreams because that isn't going to happen . . . not initially. As you're falling asleep, remind yourself that you're going to remember a dream. Then, when you wake up in the morning the first thing you need to do is remember a dream. Don't try; just do it. Write down what you remember and don't be discouraged if you only remember bits and pieces, or perhaps nothing at first. This takes practice, like any habit or skill you'd like to develop. Just be persistent and write down anything you remember because as the day progresses and you get caught up in the daily business of living, the dream will fade. Once you remember a dream think about which category might best describe it, ask yourself how you were feeling in the dream, and then consider what's going on in your life that might have precipitated the dream. That's it.

A final comment: How we feel is much more important than what we think. Thoughts can be distorted, over-analyzed, and intellectualized. Feelings are what they are and dreams are the most helpful way I know to understand our feelings and to achieve some clarity about how we respond emotionally to our feelings. This almost brings me to the chapter about feelings and emotions, but I need to talk about one other idea before I get there. Are you any good at math?

Chapter 8

E + R = O

Other people can't take credit or blame
for the outcomes of your life.

Any guesses about what E+R =O might mean? I'll give you a hint and tell you that the letter E stands for Event, and the letter O stands for Outcome. What could you add to the word Event that would equal some sort of Outcome?

Here's an example that might give you the answer: Let's say that the Event is a beach party. You're attending this party with ten other people. You aren't having much fun, so the outcome is you leaving the party early—long before anyone else leaves—and driving home alone. What would you have to add to the beach party to equal an outcome like this? If you're thinking that the answer to my question has to do with your reaction to the party, you've got it. You feel uncomfortable with the antics of several people attending the party and you leave. Your reaction to the event influences the outcome.

Event + Reaction = Outcome.

Using the same example, but substituting a different reaction, perhaps one of enjoyment and being comfortable, the outcome would be that you stay and continue to have a good time.

I've talked quite a bit about choices in many different contexts so far, and I'll continue that discussion in the next chapter when I discuss feelings and emotions, but it's important to stop a moment here and consider something very significant about the outcomes of our choices.

You're a willing participant in the events of your life. You've created those events or you've agreed to be a willing participant in an event someone else has created. How things turn out for you in terms of the outcome of those experiences depends on your reaction to the events. YOUR reaction. Let me be more specific.

Let's say that it's raining; that's the Event. Let's also say that you enjoy the rain; that's the Reaction. The Outcome of the experience of walking in the rain will be a pleasurable and positive one for you because of your reaction to the rain. Your response to the rain is the key factor in determining what the outcome of the experience will be for you. Substitute a different reaction to the rain and you'll have a different outcome.

Here's one more example and then we'll move on: Let's say that you have an important presentation to make at work; that's the Event. Your reaction to the upcoming event is that you're nervous, not at all confident, and you wish that someone else would just take over for you; that's the Reaction. The Outcome of the experience is that your presentation is not successful. How you felt about the presentation directly affected the outcome for you. If, on the other hand, you'd felt calm, confident, and willing to present, the outcome would have been very different. You influenced the outcome by your response to the situation.

The key factor in my examples is YOU. Your responses to any situation or event influence the outcome for you. Other people can't take credit or blame for the outcomes of your life any more than you can do the same for others.

I've mentioned E+R=O now because when I talk about feelings and emotions in the next chapter it's going to be very important for you to consider this equation as you think about what I have to say next. Ready?

Chapter 9

FEELINGS AND EMOTIONS

Honoring our feelings and how we respond to them is important.

No, feelings and emotions aren't the same. There are really only two feelings: love and fear. How we express those feelings is emotion. I could stop right there and this would be the shortest chapter in the book, but I'm thinking that you might like a longer explanation. Okay, let's take feelings first.

It might sound simplistic (and perhaps even inaccurate) to say that there are only two feelings, but it's true. If you come from a place of love, the way you function as a human being will be dramatically different than the way you perceive the world from a place of fear. Both love and fear provide the bottom line, and we spin-off from those two perspectives. If love is the feeling that fills you up, then all of your dealings with everyone and everything in your world will reflect that feeling. Love is non-judgmental; love is acceptance and understanding; love is respect and honor; love is altruistic; love is kindness and compassion;

love is security and positive belief; love is laughter and joy; love is trust; love is believing that you're in charge of you; love is knowing that we're all connected, and most importantly, love is the absence of fear. Fear, on the other hand, is everything that love is not. If fear motivates you there's no room for love in your life because the negative contaminates everything you think and do.

Love and fear are pure and unadulterated, but we rarely express them as they exist in their completeness because our ever-present filter systems dilute their impact, and that's where emotions come into the picture. Every emotion we express comes from either love or fear. Think about it. If you feel love for everything and every living being around you, your filter system will filter that love and you'll show emotions like compassion, trust, and acceptance. If, on the other hand, you feel afraid, your filter system will sift that fear into emotions like anxiety, lack of trust, insecurity, and judgmental attitudes.

You don't believe me? I challenge you to come up with any emotional response that isn't a filtered version of either love or fear. Go ahead; make a list. I've had this conversation with many people, and by the time we finish talking the end result is that no one has ever been able to come up with an emotion that doesn't come, either directly or indirectly, from love or fear. Doing this requires a certain degree of self-awareness on your part, though, because we often delude ourselves about what we're really feeling.

Let's take anger as an example. Anger comes from fear. If, for purposes of discussion, you feel angry because your relationship with someone has ended—for whatever reason—take a look at what's behind the anger. Fear of being rejected or betrayed? Fear of loneliness? Fear that your former significant other has found someone who is _____ (more loving, more intelligent, more beautiful . . . you supply the word) than you? Fear that you are somehow incapable of commitment? Fear that your judgment was impaired? Fear that you allowed yourself to love someone who has decided that he or she doesn't love you back? Fear that you allowed yourself to be hurt by this person? Fear that you wasted your time? Fear that your former lover walked away because you were too possessive? There are more "fear that" statements, but you get the idea. Regardless of which statement fits you, if you look at the emotional responses you indulge in because of anger (jealousy, hurt, frustration, or depression, to name a few) they all come from a base of fear.

Let's take the same example and look at it from a base feeling of love. If your relationship with someone ends, you accept that end as something that may open the door for a beginning; you accept the end without judging or blaming;

you think about what you learned from the experience; you wish your former lover well; you get on with your life.

Doesn't sound very human does it? Even though we're all capable of coming from a place of love rather than fear our human-ness often gets in the way because what makes sense in the abstract doesn't hold up under the scrutiny of day to day experiences. This is a bit like my choice illustrations in that you may have agreed with me in theory about the choice thing, but when I asked you to consider specific examples I could hear you saying, "Wait a minute. That's not right." My point here is that if we could come from a place of love rather than fear we would be more successful human beings. Just having this information might make a huge difference in the way you emotionally respond to whatever comes up in your life if you use the information in a way that allows your emotional responses to work for you instead of against you.

There's also a bit of self-awareness necessary here too. We draw to ourselves. If we feel fear, manifestations of that fear will march right to us as if they're being drawn by a magnet. When we send out fear signals, those signals draw negative experiences to us. We're in charge of sending out those signals of course, even though we may not be consciously aware that we're doing so. Conversely, if we feel love, the emotional signals that result from that feeling will resonate with positive experiences and we'll draw those to ourselves. Does that concept make sense to you?

Okay. Assuming, at least for purposes of discussion, that you buy what I'm saying, how do you remove fear and embrace love? It's all a matter of choice. You're in charge of everything about you, remember? That includes feelings and your emotional responses to those feelings. If your response to that statement is to say, "I can't help the way I feel," then my reply to you is simply, "Yes, you can." Feelings and emotions are choices too.

If you've ever used the phrase, "You hurt my feelings," in response to something that someone else has said or done, you get to stand in line with everyone else who would like to make other people responsible for their emotional responses. Can't happen. Remember E+R=O? You're in charge of how you respond to what people say and do. If your emotional response to something is to show hurt, you've chosen that response. No one else can make you respond a certain way any more than someone else can make you do something you really don't want to do. I'm not suggesting that your emotional response is always a conscious choice because our emotions don't always work that way, but you're in charge of the subconscious you too. If you choose to be hurt by what someone else says to you, look at why you need to generate that response. Look at why your filter system is responding with hurt emotions. There's always a reason—even if we don't want to look at what that reason might be—and it's really less complicated to be honest with yourself about the why behind those hurt emotions, or any emotion that's a reaction to a comment made by someone else.

Other phrases that come to mind in this discussion about feelings and emotions are ones that sound like this: "You make me happy." "You make me sad." "You make me angry." The common factor in all of these phrases is the "You make me" part. Your emotional responses to what other people say and do are your choices. If you respond happily, sadly, or angrily, you're the one responsible for those responses. To look for external explanations for your emotional responses doesn't work. I'm not saying that other people don't contribute to our emotional responses—after all, that's what interaction is all about—but I'm saying that no one can make you respond in any way you don't choose to respond. Think about what I'm saying for a minute. If you think that other people or events create your feelings of love or fear, than that makes you a kind of empty reservoir that can only be filled by other people or events. This thought also suggests that you're handing over the power behind who you are to someone else. How can that be? We all create our own reality, and if you choose to feel love, then you've created that feeling. The same thing can be said of fear. I know that you're thinking that certain events or people automatically generate fear, but there's no automatic anything. It's not a case of cause-effect. It's more a cause-choice-effect scenario that's really true. E+R=O. Works in any arena, including the one involving feelings and emotions.

Another way of considering the ideas I've talked about in this chapter is to look at the concept of control. Many people think they have no control over their emotions and that's a very comfortable place to be for them. To say that you can't help the way your emotions work for you is very safe in a sense because the "It's just the way I am" philosophy is a way of giving yourself permission to be the way you are without any pause for reflection. Of course, it's okay for us to be the way we are; who else would we be? However, most people I've worked with over the years in counseling situations don't think it's okay for them to be the way they are, especially when they're trying to understand their emotions. That out of control sensation you feel when you're having a strong emotional response is very unsettling and yet to suggest that you can control your emotional responses is also unsettling because many people want to control other people's emotional responses instead of just working with their own. The wife who wants to control how her husband responds to other women is trying to control the wrong person. She needs to look at how she responds to her husband's behavior and then work with that.

Here's a comment about emotions that you might find interesting and helpful; it was brought to my attention by a friend when we were discussing what's difficult about being human. My friend immediately responded to my question with the phrase "emotional safety." When I asked what the words meant to her she said that she's created a kind of safety zone she uses when she responds emotionally to other people, and that safety zone exists for her because of her childhood experiences. She lived with an alcoholic mother for many years, and she described her life during that time as a kind of emotional roller coaster. As a child she hadn't developed the skills to deal with her responses to her mother's problems, and so she isolated herself emotionally in order to feel safe and not vulnerable to her mother's mood swings and alcoholic behavior. As an adult she's come to realize that how she responds emotionally to some people depends on how emotionally safe she feels with them. She never felt emotionally safe with her mother, but she's finding that not all people are like her mother, yet she carries that safety net with her—just in case—and she uses it whenever she feels emotionally uncomfortable.

Her insight into this issue has given her an opportunity to take a look at whether or not she really needs the net any longer. The potential problem for her is that the safety net has become comfortable and even habitual, and she's wondering whether she's closing herself off unnecessarily sometimes. Understanding the why behind some of her emotional responses will be very helpful if she chooses to accept the idea that she's in charge of how she responds emotionally to everything.

Honoring our feelings and how we respond to them is important. It's one more aspect of being human that can be wonderful or difficult. You choose. A key element here is being honest with yourself about what you're really feeling and understanding why you respond to that feeling in the way that you do. Another case of the value of self-awareness.

Another way of looking at how we respond emotionally to our feelings is to think of emotions as conditioned or learned responses. If, for example, your emotional response to being with people who are recognized as authority figures is to immediately become defensive and insecure, you might want to take a look at the why behind your response. Is your response one that you learned—and are hanging on to—based on past experiences? If so, just saying for example, that you feel the way you do because your father yelled at you when you did something he perceived as being wrong is placing the responsibility for your feelings on the wrong person. Your response to your father didn't happen automatically. You learned to respond to him as you did for reasons that made sense to you at the time, but why continue those same responses after the fact? You can choose to learn how to respond to authority figures differently if your conditioned responses aren't working for you any longer. Why carry around baggage that you don't need? Traveling light is a good thing.

Another aspect of emotional responses that you might want to consider is the judgment value of those responses. We often attach judgments to our emotions, and because of those judgments we consider some emotional responses to be "good" and some to be "bad." For example, if shedding tears is something you don't like to do because you think that crying is a sign of vulnerability and weakness, you've attached a negative value to a very natural response to many situations. I once worked with a man who constantly fought his need to cry because he said that he was taught as a child that "big boys don't cry" and he carried that judgment with him for years. His perception was that he showed himself to be less than a man if he cried, regardless of the situation. Unfortunately, that judgment about crying carried over to other emotional responses as well, and his wife finally divorced him because she said that he refused to show his emotions about anything. This is what I call the "contamination factor." Judgments, particularly related to emotional responses, tend to contaminate, and you need to be really careful about labeling your emotional responses as being either "good" or "bad." Viewing them as being healthy or unhealthy might be more productive. There's something to be said about the Zen Buddhist approach of letting emotions come up without judgment and then letting them go without attaching yourself to them. It's an interesting exercise to do this with any emotion: let the anger rise to the surface, look at it, acknowledge its presence, and then let it go. Our emotions are constantly changing and to hang on to any one emotion for any length of time isn't very productive and requires a great deal of effort.

Let me give you a personal example of what I've just said. When my partner of forty years went on to her next expression of spirit twenty years ago I felt very sad that she wasn't physically with me any longer, and I went through a grieving process as I learned to adjust to life here without her. I did, however, function in a fairly productive way without hanging on to the sadness. I laughed, socialized, wrote, took pleasure in certain activities, and in general I experienced life in a new chapter of my visit here. I worked hard not to allow the sadness I felt to contaminate my other emotional responses. During those times when I felt overwhelmed by a sense of loss I let that emotion rise to the surface, I experienced it, and then I let it go. Doing anything less would have been attaching too much to the emotion and would, at least from my perspective, have been unhealthy at best, and would have seriously dishonored everything my late partner taught me about being human.

One final note with regard to feelings and emotions. Use your intuition for insight into why you express your emotions in the way that you do. This is another case where thinking and analyzing is a vastly over rated exercise; thinking about your feelings doesn't do much in terms of understanding them. Look to your animal friend to teach you. You know how your dog or cat feels about you even though he or she isn't expressing those feelings with words. Trust that same intuitive approach with people and how you respond to your own emotions.

Chapter 10

CAUSE AND EFFECT

. . . the effects of causes exist because of the choices
that are found in those spaces between cause and effect

I've already mentioned cause and effect, especially as
the topic relates to E+R=O, but I'd like to talk briefly
about the concept a bit more, particularly after the previous
chapter in which I suggest that you have control over your
feelings and emotions just as you do everything else. You
still aren't comfortable with that idea are you? It's okay;
these ideas may be different for you and it might take a
while to feel comfortable with them.

I've continually talked about choices in the previous
chapters because it's an important concept to consider
when you're thinking about being a healthy human being.
If you can learn to be responsible for your choices, then
you'll be functioning as the "real deal."

What's true (at least for me) is that there are no "auto-
matics" in life. There's no such thing as cause=effect. As I
said earlier, the way the cause/effect concept works is that
it's more like: choice-cause-choice-effect. Let me give you

an example of what I'm talking about and how the concept works:

Choice: You decide that you don't want to be married any longer.

Cause: Your choice to leave your spouse causes you to file for divorce. (Cause happens because of the choice that precedes it)

Choice: In the process of the many conversations that occur between you, your lawyer, your spouse, your children, and most importantly between your conscious and subconscious mind, you choose to see a counselor. Your spouse joins you in these sessions and you both come to a clearer understanding about your problems as a married couple.

Effect: You remain married and the relationship improves because you're both choosing to work on the problem areas.

You could substitute any number of choices in the above example and both the cause and the effect would change depending on the choices involved. You see what I'm getting at here? Effect doesn't immediately follow cause without choices being involved.

Here's another example on a more mundane level:

Choice: John chooses to feel angry with the referee because he thinks the referee has made an unfair call.

Cause: John's anger causes him to throw a bat at the referee. (Remember that John is in charge of his anger; he's generated the emotional response. The anger doesn't just happen.)

Choice: The referee chooses to move out of the way.

Effect: The bat doesn't harm the referee, but John gets thrown out of the game for his actions.

What follows then might be a very angry exchange between John and the referee in which words like "What were you thinking? You could have killed me!" are said by the referee.

The point here is that the effect didn't directly follow the cause because there were choices involved, most significantly by the referee. His choice to move out of the way caused him to be unharmed. John's choice to act on his anger caused him to be thrown out of the game. Two other people involved in the same scenario might have made different choices given the same perceived unfair call, and the cause and effect would change because of their choices.

On a metaphysical level, you could also probably make a case for the fact that John really didn't intend to harm the referee, but was just blowing off steam, and so his intent influenced the outcome. Intent is a very powerful motivator and deserves a closer look than we often give it. There's quite a bit of information in the area of quantum physics about intent and even how just "being" influences the effects of certain causes, but I'm not here to discuss the "observer theory," only to mention that there's plenty of scientific evidence to support the fact that just being, or observing, influences any event.

Here's one more example:

Choice: An airport mechanic chooses to do a less than thorough job of checking an airplane before the plane is scheduled to fly.

Cause: A malfunction, something that could have been avoided if the plane had been thoroughly checked, causes the plane to crash.

Choice: Everyone on the plane chose to feel fear, panic, and desperation except Frank who, during the plane's erratic descent, felt safe, secure, and saw himself at home with his family.

Effect: Everyone on the plane died except Frank who was found unharmed in a nearby field, still strapped to his seat.

The above incident actually happened several years ago, and I know you've read of similar stories including many involving natural events like tornadoes and earthquakes that appear to be very selective in the damage caused.

So, what's going on here? The answer is one that not only makes sense in the abstract, but also on a practical level if you really think about it. We make choices that determine the effects of events in which we're involved. Sometimes those choices aren't conscious, but they exist all the same. In the case of Frank, his choices weren't expressed as choices as much as they were a state of mind. I know that some would argue that Frank didn't die in the plane crash because it just wasn't "his time." The assumption here is that Frank (or anyone else) isn't in charge of his death, but he is. We all are. Death is a choice too, just like everything else. But that's another chapter.

It's convenient and sometimes easy to generalize about human behavior, but you know, perhaps from your own experience, that not everyone who experiences a difficult childhood, for example, automatically becomes a damaged adult who indulges in anti-social behavior. The effects of our background exist in ways we choose to manifest them, just as the effects of causes exist because of the choices that are found in those spaces between cause and effect.

We all create our own reality, and the choices we make influence the causes and effects that occur in our world. So, the next time you wish you were fabulously wealthy, don't forget it's the choices you make that generate that effect. And yes, winning the lottery would be nice, but you do have to buy a ticket!

Chapter 11

TIME

Use your time in ways that work positively for you.

There is no time. Time is simply a convenience we've created to organize our lives. No, I'm not just talking crazy here. Once again, this concept is substantiated in science on many levels, but I'm not concerned about science right now. I do want to talk about time, but not in a meta-physical sense . . . at least not until the end of this chapter. Since we've created time, then it might be helpful to live within the limitations we've created in the most productive way possible, which means that we need to take a look at how we use time and how our use of time can affect our lives as humans.

How you spend your time is very important. I know that sounds like another simplistic statement, and you're probably wondering what possible insight you might gain from what I've just said. Ask yourself whether you really believe that time is important, and then consider whether what you believe can be seen in your actions.

Let's take me as an example. I believe that how I spend my time is very important, and I also honor the premise that other people feel the same way about how they spend their time. If I say that I'm going to be somewhere at a particular time, I'm not late because I don't think it's responsible of me to spend someone else's time by asking them to wait for me. When I have an appointment with the dentist, I show up on time and if I'm asked to wait more than ten minutes beyond the time set by the dentist I leave because I believe that my time is just as valuable as the dentist's time. When I invite someone over for dinner, I generally allow my guests to set the time since I'm pretty flexible about what time I eat. With those conditions in play, I then expect my guests to show up at the time they've set. When I was teaching, I always provided my students with information at the beginning of the course about when papers would be due, when tests would be given, and when class would begin and end. If they asked to hand in a paper late, my answer was no. If they were not present to take a test, they were not permitted to make the test up later. If I gave a quiz at the beginning of the class and they arrived late, they missed the opportunity to earn points by taking the quiz. Inflexible? I think not. I provided my students with every bit of information they would need to do well in my class, including an explanation about why the timeline existed and what my actions would be if they chose not to play the game. Given all of the information they would need to be successful in the class, my students could then choose whether or not they wished to follow the guidelines established.

My point about time in the above examples has to do with respect and responsibility, but there's more.

You need to be clear about how you want to spend your time and then act on those thoughts. If you feel that your time is valuable, then spend it in ways that you consider to be valuable. Aimlessly wandering through a day without ever feeling like you're using your time wisely gets you frustrated. It's also a marvelous cop-out, which permits you to make statements like "I would have_____, but I just didn't have the time." Time is there for you to use; if you didn't take time to do something that was a choice on your part.

We all prioritize our actions and in doing so we inevitably end up making choices about how we spend our time. Just be sure you're aware of the choices you make with regard to how you use your time.

Often how we use or don't use our time has to do with subconscious feelings that aren't close enough to the surface for us to access them unless we really tune in to ourselves. Again, to use myself as an example: When I was younger I thought that I wanted to write a novel. I fantasized about sitting at my desk, typewriter (before computers) at the ready, just waiting for the bird of inspiration to poop profound thoughts on my head that I could mold into the great American novel. I would set aside time during an afternoon to write, but often I found myself thinking that I first needed to clean the house, take out the garbage, organize my desk, write some letters, and in general I spent my so-called writing time preparing to do something I never got around to doing. It was years later before I realized that I wasn't writing because I didn't have anything to say. I'm doing a great deal of writing now because I do feel that I have something to say, but in the case of this book, you'll have to decide for yourselves if my hypothesis is true for you. The point is that how we actually do spend our time says a great deal about what's really important to us.

This is a "walk your talk" chapter. It's all about living in the moment, learning from the past, and preparing for the future. All of that involves using time . . . even though it doesn't exist.

As an exercise to test how you really use your time, draw a circle and pretend that the circle represents a twenty-four-hour day. Think about how you spend twenty-four hours and give each activity you do during the day a visual amount of the circle that is proportionate to the amount of time you spend doing that activity. The end result will tell you something important about what you really value in terms of how you spend your time. If you end up seeing that a much smaller portion of your day is spent doing a particular activity than you would like, if this activity is really important to you then you need to find ways to prioritize your activities so you're spending as much time as you'd like doing whatever is important to you.

If you're a busy working wife and mother reading this, I'll bet that you're thinking that what I've said is all good and well, but your day is so filled with working, getting the kids to school, day care, making arrangements for them to go to soccer practice, ballet, and then coming home to prepare dinner, attending PTA meetings, keeping the house clean, etc. that there isn't possibly any way you could use your time more productively because you're overwhelmed by what needs to be done in a day, and there simply isn't enough time during a day for you to do what you really want to do. (I know that I've just written an impossibly long sentence, but I wanted to somehow sympathetically illustrate how long your day probably feels to you.) Your point is well taken, but I need to remind you of the obvious here: You chose to marry, have children, and live the life you do. It's a matter of the big choices having a ripple effect on the smaller ones that come with the territory.

The above paragraph is one that might best be viewed from the perspective of a dog. I know that this book is about being human, but some of the most valuable lessons I've learned about being human come from the dogs that have been and are an important part of my life. Dogs live in the moment. If the activities mentioned in the previous paragraph are important to you, then enjoy each one for what that experience has to offer you. While you're rushing from work to watch your son's soccer game, think about what you're doing. Remind yourself that you're doing this because you love your son and want to support an activity that's important to him. Be fully present as you anticipate the game. When you get to the game, enjoy the competition and stop thinking about what you're going to prepare for dinner. If we spend our present time thinking about the future or the past, we completely miss the moments that make memories. Don't set yourself up to be someone who says, "I wish I had only taken the time to do. . . ." You're in charge of how you spend your time, just as you are about everything else in your life.

One final note about time. I do want to explain what I meant in the first paragraph of this chapter when I said that there is no time. This is the metaphysical postscript to this chapter:

Imagine, if you will, that you're sitting at a table on

which there are several books, each open to a different chapter. The books are all there in front of you, and you can pick up any one of them to read if you choose to do so. Each life, like the books in front of you, is there for you to choose. All of those lives, like the books, exist simultaneously and it's only our choice to live a particular life that makes that life conscious and active. No, I'm not saying that those lives are all mapped out already, but they do exist within you because you are the sum total of all of your past, present, and future lives. For obvious reasons of sanity, living all of our lives consciously would be very difficult, just as trying to read many books simultaneously is not an easy task. We do, however, sometimes have what I call "bleed throughs" when a different life seeps into our consciousness. Some people would call that sensation déjà vu, but I just think of it as a momentary lapse in consciousness.

Have I confused you by what I've said about time? I think maybe I have because I can see a big question mark hovering above your head. Think about your mind and your brain. I know that many people use the words "mind" and "brain" interchangeably, but I don't think they're the same at all. Our minds are much broader in scope than our brains. Our minds aren't limited by out physical being or our consciousness. When you use the phrase "in my mind's eye" you're talking about something you see that isn't tangible. Your imagination is fueling your vision, and as I mentioned when I was talking about dreams, there are no restrictions in terms of time or place in your imagination. Use this same lateral thinking exercise when you think about time. Time has no boundaries or space limitations. All of our lives are available for us to experience; we just don't activate all of those experiences on a conscious level.

Deal with now because that's what you've come here to experience. Just acknowledge that you're much more than the sum total of your parts. Much more.

Be fully present. Use your time in ways that work positively for you.

Chapter 12

BEING CLEAR ABOUT THE MISSION

Being clear about the mission means
acknowledging your need to be connected
and then taking steps to activate that connection.

*I*f you're like most people, at some point in your life here
on Earth you feel, with varying degrees of certainty that
you're here for a reason. Sometimes you even feel like you
know specifically why you're here when you spend your
time doing something that is meaningful to you. Often,
doing certain activities will resonate with you in such a
powerful way that you say to yourself, "I was born to do
this." However, it's also possible that you're living your life
without being really clear about your mission. You may feel
that you're here for a purpose, but you haven't the foggiest
idea what that purpose might be.

This idea about being clear about the mission was also
a top vote getter in my conversations with people about
what was so difficult for them about being human. I found

very few people who didn't think that they were here for a reason, but most people I spoke with weren't at all clear about why they're here except for perhaps brief flashes of insight that didn't seem to translate into anything useful for them.

We do live purposeful lives. Everything we think, feel, and act on is purposeful and deliberate. We've chosen to be here in order to learn whatever lessons we've assigned ourselves. We are both teacher and student in a classroom that encompasses the entire playing field of Earth. We chose to be here. We live our lives based on those choices.

I know. You're thinking that if what I've said in the above paragraph is true, why then are we not always clear about our mission here? What gets in the way of our knowing what our lives are really all about? What prevents us from being successful human beings?

The answer to all of the above questions is that we get in our own way sometimes. We're too busy moving from point A to point B to be fully present and to listen to ourselves. Remember that we haven't set ourselves adrift here without still remaining connected to that part of us that remains Home. Connections only work, however, if they're activated. You can plug a lamp into an electrical outlet, but unless you turn the switch on the lamp it doesn't light up. If you don't access that part of you that remains Home while you're here experiencing life as a human being on Earth, then you live a life that is unconnected and without the purpose that you've established for yourself.

To continue with the lamp analogy, in order for the lamp to provide light certain other factors must be present: The lamp needs to be connected to wiring; the wiring needs to be connected to the electrical outlet; the outlet needs to be connected to the power source in the house; the power source in the house needs to be connected to the power pole in the street; the power pole in the street needs to be connected to a transformer; the transformer needs to be connected to the basic source of energy. Which two words have I used consistently and repetitively in the above sentence? If you said *needs* and *connected*, you get the point. Being clear about the mission means acknowledging your need to be connected and then taking steps to activate that connection.

We understand why we're here when we get the fact that we have needs and those needs must be connected in order for them to work productively. We came here because we need to learn, but learning doesn't occur in a vacuum. If we acknowledge our connections to the part of us that's Home, to Earth, to our bodies, to the people around us, to how we choose to spend our time, then we begin to get a sense about why we're here. How?

Be aware of what you're doing (or not doing) and take time to check out what that activity (or lack thereof) says about you. Here's another personal example: When I was a kid I just knew that I was going to be a doctor. Whenever any adult asked me what I was going to be (Isn't that a funny question? As if I weren't already being . . .) when I grew up, I always responded the same way. "I'm going to be a doctor." I played that tape all through high school, never noticing that I didn't do well in any kind of science class, except physics, because I wasn't even remotely interested in the subject matter. When I was in college I enrolled in a pre-med course of study. All set in cement. It wasn't until I was a junior in college that I stopped one day—in a rare moment of insight—and realized that I had no interest in Chemistry or Biology, and that I often cut those classes to play tennis. When I looked at the courses in which I'd consistently enrolled since my freshman year the majority of them involved literature and psychology. Last time I checked you don't get into medical school with a double major in English Literature and Psychology and a minor in Philosophy. Uh oh. Bottom line was, of course, that I didn't want to get into medical school. I didn't really want to be a doctor, but I never noticed that my actions, for years actually, were telling me that vital bit of information. I wasn't paying attention. The realization that I didn't really want to be a doctor was difficult because I almost felt betrayed by myself. I wasn't savvy enough to realize that I'd known what I was doing all along, and so it took some adjusting on my part to re-focus my energy and move in a direction that involved literature and human behavior.

Pay attention. Watch what you're doing. We really do know what we're doing, but sometimes we don't notice that we're following a particular path until we've reached a point that causes us to notice where we are and what we're doing.

There's also something to be said here for flexibility. Sometimes a particular path takes us to another that seems more appealing, and so we change direction. Notice what gets your attention. If you work in an office but find that you spend all of your free time volunteering at an animal shelter and can hardly wait until you get off work to go there, look at what you're doing. Notice that you have a connection with the animals at the shelter. Think about what that connection feels like and what the experience says about how you like spending your time. If you find yourself not looking forward to going to your job in the office take some action to translate your volunteering at the shelter into something that will pay you money. When I was counseling students about careers my favorite line was always, "Think about how you like to spend your time and then figure out a way to get paid for doing that." Makes sense to me. How about you?

Here's an exercise that I've often used in counseling people about noticing what's important to them. If you're going to do this right now it's important that you follow my directions exactly in terms of when to read the next instruction:

Take three sheets of paper and label them <u>Past</u>, <u>Present</u> and <u>Future</u> respectively. Without using words, represent your past, present and future on each of the pieces of paper. I'm not going to be any more specific than that. You need a box of crayons, felt pens, different colored chalk, whatever you have at hand. This isn't a test of your artistic ability, so don't be concerned that you can't draw. I've done this often just as a reality check for myself, and I'm the Queen of Stick Figures, believe me. Don't agonize about what to draw; just move your pen as fast as the ideas come to you. No one else will see what you've done unless you choose to show your drawings to someone. Don't think; just draw as fast as you can without editing or analyzing. Include as many visual representations of each time in your life that you like. When the ideas stop coming, it's time to quit. You shouldn't spend any more than twenty minutes doing the whole exercise.

Now . . . this is very important:

DON'T READ ANY FURTHER UNTIL YOU'VE COMPLETED THE EXERCISE.

Finished? Okay, continue reading.

When you've represented your past, present and future, take a look at what you've done and ask yourself what you've just said (without using words) about what's important to you and how that translates into what your mission here might be. Given the fact that you have your whole life to choose from in terms of what you represent, what you've chosen to show as being important to you is significant. I know that I didn't ask you to represent important stuff, but trust me; if you drew it, it's important. Ask yourself these questions:

1. Do your three drawings represent people, places, events, or emotions? Your answer here will tell you what's most important to you about your life.

2. Are your representations primarily positive or negative? What does your answer here tell you?

3. Have you represented yourself in the drawings at all? If so, what are you doing? If not, where are you?

4. Is your future as specifically represented as your past and present, or is your visual representation of this part of your life more abstract? Why or why not?

5. If I asked you to look at each drawing and pick out the single most significant thing represented in each drawing, what would you pick? Why?

6. Have you used colors, and if so is there any significance to what color you've used for specific representations? If you only used a black or blue pen/pencil why didn't you use any other colors?

7. Have you represented emotions in any of the drawings?

8. Look at the sheet of paper representing your future. How much of your past and present is there? This one is really important because whatever you choose to represent as your future will tell you how important those things/people/emotions are to you, but if there's no evidence of anything in your past or present that relates to the future you see for yourself, then you need to ask yourself why you aren't making your future happen.

9. Which of the three was the most difficult for you to do? Why?

10. Stand back and look at all three sheets. Are there lots of images on each sheet? Only a few? Notice how you've organized your life and think about what that might say to you.

11. After you've studied each sheet, write down a summary of how you see your past, present and future based on what you've drawn.

12. Ask yourself this question: "What is my mission and what am I doing to make that mission real to me?"

13. If you feel up to getting an interpretation from someone besides yourself, show your three sheets of paper to someone, and without directing this person in any way, ask the person to whom you're showing the drawings to tell you what they see and what they think the drawings mean. Sometimes how we see ourselves isn't the same as how others see us, and you might be interested in checking if your perception about who you are and what's important to you comes across to someone else.

Bottom line here? Think about where you've been, where you are, and where you're going. Somewhere in all of that thinking and feeling your mission here will surface and become clear to you.

Chapter 13

AGING

Some of the lessons you've chosen to learn
in this life may only present themselves to you
for consideration at certain times in your life.

Since I've just finished talking about past, present and future (even though there is no time) it might be appropriate at this point to talk a bit about aging. This aspect of being human is another topic that came up again and again when I talked with people about the difficulties involved in being human.

For some people the aging process is one that proves to be *very* difficult for many reasons. I did, however, find a consistent pattern that evidenced itself in the lives of those people who were concerned about aging. People who were most concerned about aging lived primarily in the past, at least in their minds. This is what I call the "aging cheerleader syndrome." Women who were concerned about aging wore what might be described as an excessive amount of make-up, worked hard to maintain a certain body weight, and in general they wanted to look just like they did when they were in high school. I even spoke with one woman who only kept photographs of herself when she was much younger. Men who had the same concerns wore clothes that might have looked better on younger men, often dyed their hair to hide gray streaks, and in general they wanted to look like they did when they were younger too.

The why behind being concerned about aging is complicated because there are many emotions at work here. I think it's safe to say that we do understand that our bodies will age with time, but often there's an unwillingness to accept this fact because somehow many people feel that who they are is measured by their appearance. There's that external validation thing that I've talked about earlier. Also, aging for many people represents a passing of time that reminds them that they may not have accomplished what they hoped with their lives. For many people aging is a reminder that their bodies will die, and they don't want to even think about that. The emotions that come into play here are insecurity, frustration, obsession, and all kinds of other negative emotions that can be attributed to one feeling: fear.

You knew I was going to say that, didn't you? If you're remembering the chapter on feelings and emotions, you'll recall that I said that there were only two feelings: love and fear. Concern about aging can only come from fear.

Let's take a closer look at this concern. I'm using the word "concern" here because it's a fairly bland word that can conjure up a variety of responses, depending on the degree of concern. You'll have to decide for yourself where your concerns about aging, if you have any, fall into place.

Culturally, we live in a society, at least here in the United States, which celebrates youth and beauty. Going into detail about this phenomenon really isn't necessary because you know what I mean, don't you? Somehow the barometer that measures our success about being human is one in which a youthful appearance is important. Seems to me that the old cliché about "inner beauty" might be considered in this context as being a valid alternative to external appearance, but then you'll have to decide whether or not that consideration works for you.

If you're afraid of growing old, look at why that fear exists for you. What exactly is it that you're afraid of here? Are you afraid that people won't care as much about/for you if you age? Are you afraid that you won't be successful in your career if you grow older? Are you afraid that your body will begin to fall apart as you age? Are you afraid that you won't be able to do the things that are important to you if your body ages? Are you afraid that aging automatically means that you will be less productive as a human being? Are you afraid that you will lose your independence as you grow older? Are you afraid aging places you that much closer to dying?

I could go on and on with questions, but my point here is that if you're concerned about aging it might be a good idea to look at the why behind that concern and evaluate what that fear says about you.

So, just how do you age gracefully and positively without allowing fear to contaminate your sense of who you are? I have several suggestions:

First and perhaps most importantly, live in the moment. Participate in every aspect of your life, regardless of how old you are. If you don't look like you did when you were younger, acknowledge the person you are now when you look in the mirror and celebrate your human-ness at this moment in your life. Don't spend time regretting the fact that you don't look as young as you did twenty years ago, because it's a waste of time and energy. Enjoy who you are right now. Today.

A second suggestion would be to live positively and productively, doing whatever you can to stay healthy. Please notice that I said "healthy" not "young." You chose your body, and it's important to take care of that body as best you can during every phase of your visit here. I'm not talking about obsessive health nut behavior here, but rather reasonable care of the suit of armor. Don't allow the metal to rust, but you don't need to polish it all the time either.

A third thought would be to use what you see as your own personal aging process as a way for you to evaluate how successful you've been in terms of accomplishing your goals. If you wake up one morning and realize that you're fifty-seven years old and you haven't done some of the things you've said you wanted to do, then get moving and start doing what you want to do.

A fourth suggestion would be to not obsess about diseases that often accompany aging. Remind yourself that you're in charge of your body and disease will not invade your suit of armor unless you welcome its presence. Still not sure about that, are you? All I can say at this point is to remind you that everything is a choice. Even genetic predispositions to certain diseases don't represent automatic illnesses. (Remember: choice-cause-choice-effect.)

Fifth: Pay attention. Pay attention to your body and how you're responding to the aging process. If you look in the mirror and see gray hair and a few wrinkles, notice how you respond to those physical characteristics. If you freak out and immediately buy hair coloring solutions and sign up for Botox treatments, notice what those actions say about your priorities and what's important to you. Does having gray hair and wrinkles really make you less important as a human being?

Sixth: Understand that you can still function productively as an older person. So what if your tennis game isn't as sharp as it was when you were younger. You can still play—and even win—if that's important to you. Moderation.

Finally, don't assume that aging and unhappiness are linked together. They can be if you indulge in some of the emotions and behaviors I've mentioned in this chapter, but to assume that because your body is aging you won't be happy is a false assumption. You create your own happiness, remember?

It's very important to acknowledge and embrace the mind/body connection in this context of aging. It's only your body that ages; mentally, emotionally, spiritually, psychically, you are always whole and healthy . . . unless you choose not to be for whatever reason.

The aging process is also important to think about because some of the lessons you've chosen to learn in this life may only present themselves to you for consideration at certain times in your life if you live in a body. A friend once said that the best part about aging is the accumulation of experiences, knowledge, and the depth of living made possible because of that accumulation. As your body ages your experiences may change, and with those changes opportunities to learn that weren't available to you when you were younger may surface for your consideration. It's all about readiness to learn.

Chapter 14

DYING AND DEATH

*. . . death is a necessary process that must occur
before we can move on.*

Death, as we commonly think of it, doesn't exist. Just as a traditional concept of birth implying a beginning—before which there was nothing—is impossible. Death, implying an end, is equally impossible. There is no end. More appropriately, death is a change. Transformation. It's a culmination, which in the very nature of its purpose, is significant and necessary. When we've learned our lessons our bodies die, and we move on to our next expression of spirit.

We have such odd attitudes toward death in our culture. Even with a traditional Christian concept of life after death, the dying event is viewed so traumatically and often so fearfully.

I'm not suggesting that death isn't traumatic; of course, it is. Any major change is traumatic, and death is perhaps one of the most major changes we experience, but if we understand the process of being human a bit more, which is what this book is all about, I think we might understand the dying process a little better too.

Nature is a great teacher, but I wonder why we don't pay closer attention to the seasons. Think about the growth, change, dying and regeneration that we see in nature during the course of just one year, and then consider how important each facet of the cycle is in order for new life to emerge.

I know that it's all well and good to philosophize about death and dying with regard to the seasons, but when you or some member of your family is dying, things become very personal, immediate, and your perspective is distorted. I suppose it's difficult at best to be objective about one's own death, although I've met a few people who are, but if we could achieve some degree of objectivity to understand the process we might remove some of the fear attached to the experience.

Death is, however, really very personal—like birth—because only you can experience this change in your own way. During our visit here as humans we meet people who have had similar life experiences, and we can draw upon those experiences as a way to clarify our own, or we can draw upon our own past experiences to help us understand what we're doing, but death is different. Or at least it seems to be. No one can tell you how to leave your body. It's not exactly like getting advice from someone about how to tune the engine of your car; we all experience the death of our bodies in our own way and death too is a choice.

You knew I was going to say that, didn't you? I hope so, because after reading the previous chapters you should be finding me pretty predictable and consistent by now. If everything about us is a matter of choice, including our birth and how we live our lives as humans, why should death be different?

We choose everything about our body's death experience: when, where, how, why . . . everything. I can hear you saying, "Okay, with suicide what you say makes sense. The choice is clearly made." The only difference between suicide and any other kind of death is that in suicide the choice is conscious, and in most other forms of dying the choice is made on a subconscious level. Our subconscious mind, wonderful memory bank that it is, is linked so closely with that part of us that remains at Home that it knows when it's time to leave. Consciously we don't always agree and we fight, but when the choice is made we're responsible for that choice. Acknowledging both the conscious and subconscious choices we make about the death of our bodies is very important to remember.

However, the choice to die isn't always necessary when the opportunity to leave exists. Like illness, dying is often a manifestation that can be altered if other choices or alternatives are taken and seen as possible. No doubt you've heard about people who experience "miraculous" healing, and their bodies don't die in spite of medical prognosis. What's happening in these cases is that people experiencing illness and potential death from that illness make choices—on both a conscious and subconscious level—to remain in their bodies because they feel they haven't learned what they came here to learn. On the other hand, many doctors feel that their most difficult moments in facilitating healing occur when they realize that there isn't any kind of medical treatment that will prevent a person from dying if the patient is ready to leave. The efforts of medical intervention prove frustrating and meaningless, but in many cases the energy we direct toward dying can be altered—if we choose to do so—and another way to learn the lesson can be achieved.

How often have you heard people use the phrase "It was his/her time"? I think that there actually may be a "right" time to die . . . at least from a subconscious perspective. When the time is right sometimes we know and there's an acceptance that paves the way for the next stage of growth, but all too often our conscious mind refuses to accept death, and then we find ourselves arriving Home in a state of confusion. Once we're Home reflection is necessary, and with help we can see why we've chosen to leave at that particular time.

For those who believe that we live only one life here on Earth, why we choose to die is simple. The body wears out; the engine wears down and eventually stops. The suit of armor falls apart. For people like me who believe that we go on from here, death is a necessary process that must occur before we can move on.

I think we choose to die for several reasons: Sometimes we "bail out" because we find the lessons too difficult, and we don't want to face the experiences necessary in the learning process so we die. That choice can be made consciously or subconsciously, but it's important to consider that if we bail out before we've learned what we've come here to learn, we might choose to do the visit again. The lessons we've chosen for ourselves don't just disappear, and if we ignore them on one visit we may find ourselves returning to take another shot at learning what we've decided is important to learn. It's just like school. Some subjects are very difficult for people and they avoid them. The avoidance doesn't dissipate the need to learn; the process just takes longer.

Another reason we choose to leave our bodies has to do with lessons learned and mission accomplished. If we've learned what we need to know, we move on to other lives, other lessons, other deaths. This concept is particularly difficult to understand when we think of the death of a child. We view children as innocent victims of death and the untimely (from the observer's point of view) death of a child seems unfair. The choice, however, is still made—even in the mind of a child—and based on my own experiences with children who are dying, they seem to understand this far better than adults. There is an acceptance possible with children that often becomes complicated as we grow older. Perhaps because they're young and their conscious awareness hasn't become so totally encompassing, children can still remember where they've been and it's easier for them to return Home.

Another reason for death exists in the effect of an individual's death on those around him or her. We often provide learning experiences for others—if they choose to acknowledge them—and in these cases the death of an individual (or group of individuals) may have a profound effect on those with whom they've come in contact. Think about 9-11, the Holocaust, or even COVID. Sometimes we can learn about life through the deaths of others.

How we die is a factor to be considered in the same way that how we are born is significant. Death may be sudden, prolonged, painful, painless, violent, peaceful . . . any way we choose. Of course, it's easy to see why we would choose a painless death, but why a painful one? Why a long term illness, culminating in the death of the body? Again, our choices involve where we've been and where we're going. Dying is often the most difficult of all lessons, and if we handled the dying badly in one lifetime we may choose to learn to "do it better." Sometimes the how of death is profoundly influenced by our resistance, or lack of resistance, to the process. If subconsciously we've made the choice and yet we resist that choice consciously there may be pain and suffering. We need to "tune in" to our subconscious with regard to death in the same way that we need to listen to ourselves with regard to being human. If death is sudden and there is no conscious realization of what's happening, there will be a period of time spent sleeping. I suppose the sleep is necessary for our earth bodies and that part of us that always remains Home to catch up to each other, just as rest is necessary in our life here as humans. Isn't it wonderful that some things don't change no matter where we are?

I've spent a great deal of time with people whose bodies are dying, and how that experience is handled by not only the person preparing to leave, but family and friends, is as varied as the people I've known. There is, however, a common denominator in the dying experience of many people that is worth mentioning here because that perspective makes a huge difference in whether or not the process is a positive one filled with feelings of love rather than fear. The common denominator? Think about the previous chapters and particularly about the concept that runs through this book and you'll have the answer. If your answer to my question is a six-letter word beginning with C and ending with e, you've got it.

I'm thinking at this point that you may be experiencing an emotional response of anger to my talking about death as a choice. Are you? Think about why the idea of the death of the body being a choice makes you angry. If you've recently had someone you love leave their body, my saying that the death experience was a choice on their part may churn up an anger response in you because you can't imagine why your loved one would choose to leave you. Perhaps I can gently remind you here that someone else's death experience isn't about you. Let me use myself as an example:

I've already mentioned that my partner of forty years left her body about twenty years ago. We had a wonderful life together and neither of us was consciously ready for her to leave, but she knew on a subconscious/psychic level that her work was finished and she needed to move on. I didn't take her choice to move on to her next expression of spirit as a rejection of me and our life together because I knew, as did she, that her lessons were complete and we would be together again on another visit somewhere. I accepted her choice as being a necessary one for her and I knew that her decision wasn't about me. I know where she is and that knowing is a comfort to me as I re-define my life without her physical presence. I know too that my ability to live a productive life without her is a tribute to what she's taught me, and my being able to find something positive in every day honors her and the love we shared for so many years. Her need to leave when she did was all about her, but our life together, including the lessons that we learned together, was all about the *us* that always remains.

Knowing that you're in charge of everything you choose to experience as a human being—including the death of your body—is a very powerful bit of knowledge. Use that knowledge to celebrate being human and to also acknowledge that you need to move on to your next expression of spirit when you're ready to make that transition.

Chapter 15

PERCEPTION

*Or, maybe what you see doesn't really have
to be just one thing.*

You thought the last chapter might be the end of the book, didn't you? I suppose it could have been, but before we have our final cup of coffee or tea I'd like you to consider all of what I've said under the general concept of perception.

I'm thinking about insight and understanding of a very personal nature here. Your perception is unique in that it reflects only your view, which often is not shared by others.

A view shared by others is considered to be reality . . . at least that seems to be the criteria used these days. If, for example, you say that the grass is green and everyone else says that the grass is red, the red grass is considered to be reality, and your green grass isn't perceived by others to be real. Reality is just a perception agreed upon by consensus. Or, is it? I've mentioned several times in this book that we all create our own reality, but I'm wondering if that idea really makes sense to you, or if you think that it sounds right, but you have no clue at all what I'm talking about. Hold that thought.

No doubt you've seen the classic example of visual perception often used in psychology that is represented at the beginning of this chapter. Do you see an urn, or do you see two faces in profile? Once you see the faces, can you still see the urn? Perhaps you can switch back and forth, but is it difficult to re-capture the image of the urn once you've seen the two faces? Is the image an urn or two faces? Which is it? Can it be both? If so, how can that be? Or . . . maybe what you see doesn't really have to be just one thing.

You're wondering where I'm going with all of this, aren't you? Actually, I'm not going anywhere. I'm right here.

Now it's your turn to be here. To be fully present in the life you've chosen for yourself.

In many ways, this book has really been all about perception. I've told stories and offered comments about the various ways you can perceive yourself as a human being. I've asked you to think about how you function as a person and to consider the perception that you might be more than just one individual.

Your ability to acquire, interpret, select and organize information using your senses and your mind allows you to perceive the world in a way that makes sense to you. If this book offers different perceptions than you're accustomed to using, perhaps it might be fun to see if you can create a reality that includes some of those perceptions. Why would you do that? Certainly not because my view is right and yours is wrong. Oh, no. There's no right or wrong here. What I'm saying is that the world you've chosen to live in might make a different kind of sense to you if you were to consider altering your perceptions. Who knows? Your reality could be more productive, successful, interesting, joyful . . . you supply whatever word expresses your need, if you were to modify your perceptions a bit to accommodate what you've chosen to learn and to honor the choices you make as you visit here. You might even create your own personal field guide. Or, perhaps even more to the point, you might find yourself walking your talk in a reality that you've joyfully created to experience what you're learning.

It's all about lessons.

Chapter 16

FINAL THOUGHTS

*I*t feels a bit like the previous chapter really should be the end of this book, but the teacher in me can't resist conducting a little review here. At the beginning of the book I talked about what I hoped you might learn from our conversations about being human, and now I want to hit you with a series of one-liners that sum up what I hope you've learned from the book. If you want to think along with me, just go back to the Table of Contents and look at the title of each chapter. Let's see if you come up with the same list I'm about to give you. Go ahead; make your list first and then read mine. Then we'll compare notes. Ready?

- Establish a connection with the planet on which you've chosen to live.

- Embrace being human by enjoying your body and taking care of it.

- Everything is a choice.

- Be clear in your communication with all living beings.

- Understand that relationships are complicated and you only have control over what you bring to the party.

- Consider the patterns that present themselves in your life.

- Pay attention to your dreams.

- Event+Reaction=Outcome

- There are only two feelings: love and fear. Notice how your emotions express those feelings.

- Choice-cause-choice-effect

- There is no time except what we've created, so use your creation wisely.

- You can learn to be clear about your mission here by reflecting on your past, present and future.

- The body ages; you are always whole and healthy.

- Death is only a change of consciousness.

- What you see is what you see… Maybe.

Are we dancing to the same tune? If what you wrote down is similar to what I've just presented, then you've learned something from reading this book. Now the real test is to see if you can create your own personal field guide and walk your talk by experiencing what you've learned.

Celebrate being human.

ABOUT THE AUTHOR

*D*uring the course of her forty-six year teaching career Ardeth De Vries has taught high school, college, university, and adult education classes. She has offered seminars and workshops for hospitals, hospice personnel, and the general public on a variety of topics ranging from literature, psychology, spirituality, dreams, self-esteem, death/dying and animal welfare.

As an animal welfare advocate, Ardeth's work with animals includes: walking dogs and spending time with cats at a local animal shelter, fifty years of rescuing abused and neglected dogs, and serving as end-of-life consultant, animal loss counselor, newsletter editor, writer, blog mistress, Board president, and Executive Director for Old Dog Haven, a nonprofit organization that offers hospice care, assisted living and placement assistance for unadoptable senior dogs in western Washington.

Ardeth's first book, *First Light: Animal Voices in Concert,* (2006, Publishing Works) is a collection of stories about what animals teach us. Many of the dogs featured in the book are shelter dogs that once were guests at the WAIF shelter in Coupeville, Washington.

A Space Between (2011, River Sanctuary Publishing) is a metaphysical novel about possibilities, lessons and perception.

Old Dog Haven: Every Old Dog Has a Story to Tell (2014, Bennett & Hastings) is a celebration of hope, transformation and life lessons taught by old dogs and the people who love them.

When I Grow Old I Will Wear Flowers: Thoughts About Senior Dogs (2024, Bennett & Hastings) is a series of essays about living with and loving senior dogs and understanding what they teach us.

Ardeth lives in Coupeville Washington with her partner and current family of five senior rescue dogs.

A percentage of all proceeds earned by the author from this book (or any book she's written) are donated to animal welfare organizations.

www.ingramcontent.com/pod-product-compliance
Lightning Source LLC
Chambersburg PA
CBHW031201270326
41931CB00006B/357